Marty Bergen

Bergen Books
9 River Chase Terrace
Palm Beach Gardens, FL 33418-6817

First Edition published 2003.
Printed in the United States of America.
10 9 8 7 6 5 4 3 2 1

First Printing: October, 2003

Library of Congress Control Number: 2003096195

ISBN 0-9716636-9-6

Dedication

To bridge

The best game ever invented.

BRIDGE BOOKS BY MARTY BERGEN

Thanks To:

Layout, cover design, and editing by
Hammond Graphics.

My very special thanks to: Cheryl Angel,
Cheryl Bergen, Gary Blaiss, Trish and John L. Block,
Ollie Burno, Pete Filandro, Jim Garnher, Terry Gerber,
Lynn and Steve Gerhard, Pat and Gordon Gray,
Marilyn and Malcolm Jones, Steve Jones, Doris Katz,
Al Kimel, Danny Kleinman, Alex Martelli,
Harriet and David Morris, Phyllis Nicholson,
Mary and Richard Oshlag, Helene Pittler,
Sally and Dave Porter, David Pollard,
Mark Raphaelson, Jesse Reisman, Carl Ritner,
Mark Rosenholz, John Rudy, Maggie Sparrow,
Tom Spector, Merle Stetser, Bobby Stinebaugh,
and John Tripp.

FYI

1. On opening lead, we lead A from AK.

2. The player with the bidding decision to make
   is indicated by three question marks: ???
   For consistency, South is always that player,
   and his hand is the one displayed.

3. Every bidding diagram begins with West.

West	North	East	South
—	—	—	2♡
All Pass			

   The dashes are place holders, and in the example
   above, show that the auction did not begin with
   West, North, or East. The dealer was South.
   The "—" does not indicate a "Pass."

CONTENTS

Part I - Bidding

Section 1: Here and There

Section 2: We Open the Bidding

Section 3: They Open the Bidding

Part II - Card Play

Impressive Declarer Play

CONTENTS...CONTINUED

The Defense Never Rests

Part III - Back of Book

Appendix

Highly Recommended
Pages 187-192

MARTY SEZ 3 BIDDING STYLE

Opening Bids

Five-card majors.
Light opening bids, based on the Rule of 20.
1NT opening bid = 15-17 HCP.
2NT opening bid = 20-21 HCP.
2♣ opening is strong, artificial, and forcing.
Weak two-bids in diamonds, hearts, and spades.
Preempts may be light.

Responding

Limit raises — all suits.
After notrump: Jacoby Transfers and Stayman.

Slam Bidding

Blackwood — traditional, not Roman Key Card.

Competitive

Michaels Cue-Bid, Unusual Notrump.

Chapter 1:

A Whole New World

West	West	East	East
♠ Q 10 3	1♣	1♠	♠ 7 5 4 2
♡ A 6 5 2	2♠	Pass	♡ K 7 3
♢ A			♢ Q J 2
♣ K J 8 7 4			♣ Q 10 2

What a horrible contract! Before reading on, what do you think went wrong here?

Was West wrong to bid 2♠? Absolutely not. He didn't want to rebid 1NT with a side singleton. As for 2♣, **rebidding a 5-card suit should always be avoided when partner might have to pass with a singleton or void.** No, raising to 2♠ with three spades headed by two honors was West's correct rebid.

The problem was East's *normal* spade response. East's hand was screaming "notrump," as opposed to "spades." Even if opener had four spades, East would *not* have been eager to declare a spade contract. East should have ignored his lousy spades and bid 1NT.

After a 1NT response, West would have been in a win-win position. Because **a 1NT response to 1♣ guarantees a balanced hand,** West could rebid clubs without worrying that East hated that suit. Or, he might pass 1NT. Either 2♣ or 1NT would have made easily.

THE HECK WITH THE RULES

Some would refer to the following as heresy. However, as the previous page suggests, **Marty Sez:**

With a terrible 4-card major, 4-3-3-3 distribution, and a modest hand, responder should bypass the major and respond 1NT.

Partner opens 1♣ and your RHO passes. You hold:

♠ K Q 10   ♡ 5 4 3 2   ◇ K J 4   ♣ 9 8 5

Why do I believe that 1NT is the correct response?

- Your only 4-card suit is pitifully weak.

- Even if you find a fit, 4-3-3-3 hands provide no benefits in a suit contract.

- You have stoppers in two unbid suits.

- You have the right strength for a 1NT response. 1NT limits your hand, and gives a very good description of your hand in one bid. 1♡ doesn't.

Could a 1NT response work out badly? It *is* possible. *If* opener has four hearts *and* a very distributional hand, you *might* have been better off in a heart contract. Sounds like a lot of "what if's" to me.

With a terrible 4-card major, 4-4-3-2 distribution, and a modest hand, responder *might* bypass the major and respond 1NT.

Is this going too far? You tell me. Partner opens 1◇ and your RHO passes. You hold:

♠ K J 7 ♡ 9 6 5 4 ◇ Q 7 ♣ J 9 5 4

For the reasons already stated, I'd respond 1NT rather than 1♡ every day of the week, and twice on Sunday.

Here's a hand from a recent team game.

West	West	East	East
♠ Q 9 8 6	1◇	1♠	♠ 7 5 4 2
♡ —	4♡*	4♠	♡ A Q
◇ K Q J 8 7 5	Pass		◇ 10 6 2
♣ A K J			♣ Q 5 4 3

*splinter bid

Although spades split 3-2, 4♠ had no play – East lost three spades and the ◇A. The other East bypassed his spade "suit" and landed in 3NT. He won the heart lead, set up diamonds, and scored up 10 tricks. Case closed.

By the way: If your partnership agrees to sometimes ignore a very weak 4-card major and respond 1NT, that is *not* alertable.

Light 1NT overcalls when non-vulnerable allow you to take action with some otherwise unbiddable hands.

With neither side vulnerable, you pick up:

♠ A Q 2   ♡ K 4   ◇ K Q 10 4   ♣ 8 7 6 3

Not a bad hand. You're all set to open 1◇ when your RHO opens 1♠. Uh oh. With only two hearts, a double is out, and you can't overcall at the two level in a 4-card suit. A 1NT overcall promises at least 15 HCP, so that's out, too. I suppose you *have* to pass.

If you hate passing with that hand, so do I. Here's my suggestion. It's based on a lot of very positive experience. **When your side is *not* vulnerable, define a 1NT overcall as 14-17 HCP.**

Are there any risks? Of course, but no more than any other overcall. You're still at the one level, and partner knows a lot more about your hand than if you pass. What happens if partner has nothing? You may or may not survive, but I doubt that the outcome would be any different if you had the ♣J instead of the ♣8.

With a good hand, bidding now often resolves difficult guesses later on. It's also true that excessive passing and/or worrying is no fun.

Your RHO opens 1♡. Neither side is vulnerable.
Playing 1NT overcalls as 14-17 HCP, what's your call?

♠ A 4 ♡ K J 9 ◇ Q 7 6 4 3 ♣ A 10 4
Bid 1NT, not 2◇. To say that I prefer 1NT to 2◇ is the
understatement of the year.

♠ Q 5 4 ♡ Q J 6 ◇ Q J 5 2 ♣ K Q J
Pass. I'm certainly not advocating a 1NT overcall on
every balanced hand with 14 HCP and a heart stopper.
This mess is really worth about 11 points.

♠ Q 9 8 ♡ A 2 ◇ A Q 7 5 ♣ Q 6 4 3
Double. Having only three spades is not reason enough
to avoid the normal takeout double.

♠ K 8 ♡ A Q ◇ A J 9 3 ♣ 9 7 5 4 2
Bid 1NT. The two doubletons should not prevent you
from overcalling 1NT.

♠ A K 10 9 ♡ A 6 4 ◇ 6 3 ♣ K 7 5 3
Bid 1♠. With such good spades, and only one heart
stopper, the 4-card overcall is the best option.

By the way: If you decide to try lighter 1NT overcalls,
simply write "14-17 nonvul, 15-18 vul" on your
convention card under "DIRECT NT OVERCALLS."
No alert or special announcement is needed.

5-3-3-2 hands are not worth much if your 5-card suit is trump. Having no long *or* short outside suits is a liability in a suit contract.

West	West	East	East
♠ K Q J 8 5	1♠	2♠	♠ A 9 2
♡ A K	4♠	Pass	♡ J 10 9
◇ Q 6 3			◇ 7 5 4 2
♣ A 7 2			♣ K 6 3

West lost three diamonds and a club. With his 5-3-3-2, he should rebid 3NT to give responder a choice. With *his* 4-3-3-3, East would pass 3NT, and nine tricks were easy. If East had a shapely hand, he'd go back to 4♠.

West	West	East	East
♠ A J	1♣	1♡	♠ 7 2
♡ 8 7 5 4	2♡	4♡	♡ A K Q J 2
◇ K J 4	Pass		◇ Q 7 6
♣ K J 4 2			♣ 8 5 3

East had an "opening bid opposite an opening bid," and jumped to game once West raised hearts. In 4♡, East lost 1 spade, 1 diamond, and 2 clubs – down one. With his balanced hand, East should have contented himself with 3♡. West had "too many jacks," and should decline the invitation.

5-3-3-2 is an okay distribution for notrump, or when another suit is trump.

West	West	East	East
♠ K Q J	1♢	1NT	♠ 6 4 2
♡ K J 2	2NT	3NT	♡ A 10 3
♢ A J 10 9	Pass		♢ 8 2
♣ K 7 4			♣ Q J 9 8 5

East had only 7 HCP, but appreciated his nice 5-card suit. 3NT was a good contract, and East set up clubs and scored up his game.

West	West	East	East
♠ A K J 5 3	1NT	2♢*	♠ Q 4
♡ K 10 6	2♡	2NT	♡ A Q 9 8 5
♢ 5 2	4♡	Pass	♢ 10 9 4 3
♣ A 7 4			♣ 8 6

*Jacoby Transfer

East invited game with 2NT. West had only 15 HCP, but appreciated his nice 5-card suit and jumped to game. With normal splits, 11 tricks came rolling in.

Make Him an Offer He Can't Refuse

To say that bridge partners always see eye-to-eye on the best way to do things would be as ridiculous as making that same statement about life partners. However, you may become frustrated if you're dying to play a certain convention and your partner can't see the light.

Too often, each player tries to convince the other of the wisdom of *his* preference. This is rarely productive. In fact, it can even damage the relationship.

Here's my recommendation. I can honestly say that, over the years, I've had very good results with the following approach. Make partner this offer:

"Do it my way for now. However, the first time we have a disaster, I agree to switch to your way for a whole year."

Am I willing to guarantee that this will cure all of your partnership woes? Of course not. You *might* end up agreeing to play a convention that is not your first choice. On the other hand, if your favorite methods are half as good as you think they are, you may just succeed in improving the partnership, and getting things done "your way."

P.S. Whether or not your significant other plays bridge, making a similar offer at home is not a bad idea, either.

Chapter 2:

We Bid Notrump

On each of these hands, the auction has begun:

West	North	East	South
Pass	1NT	Pass	2♣
Pass	2♠	Pass	???

Does North's 2♠ bid deny four hearts? It depends on your partnership agreement. On these six hands, it makes no difference.

As South, evaluate your hand and decide what to bid. Both sides are vulnerable. **Marty Suggests:** On all quizzes, write down your answers before reading on.

1.　♠ 6 4 3　♡ K J 4 2　♢ A 9 5 4　♣ J 3

2.　♠ 7 5　♡ K 10 9 8　♢ A J 10 9 7　♣ 5 3

3.　♠ A Q 9　♡ Q 6 4 3　♢ 7　♣ 7 6 5 4 2

4.　♠ Q 9 8 3　♡ 10 6 3　♢ A J 9 7 2　♣ 3

5.　♠ J 5 4 2　♡ 7 4　♢ Q J 6 5　♣ K Q J

6.　♠ K 10 8 7　♡ 6 4　♢ A J 9 7 5　♣ 6 3

West	North	East	South
Pass	1NT	Pass	2♣
Pass	2♠	Pass	???

1. ♠ 6 4 3 ♡ K J 4 2 ◇ A 9 5 4 ♣ J 3

Bid 2NT. A normal hand for this auction.

2. ♠ 7 5 ♡ K 10 9 8 ◇ A J 10 9 7 ♣ 5 3

Bid 3NT, not 2NT. Your lovely diamonds and many
intermediates make this a lot better than hand #1.

3. ♠ A Q 9 ♡ Q 6 4 3 ◇ 7 ♣ 7 6 5 4 2

Pass, don't bid 2NT. What will you do for tricks after
a likely diamond lead? Setting up your 5-card club suit
might take months.

4. ♠ Q 9 8 3 ♡ 10 6 3 ◇ A J 9 7 2 ♣ 3

Bid 3♠. If opener had bid 2◇ or 2♡, you planned to
pass. But now that you found a spade fit, your hand
improved dramatically.

5. ♠ J 5 4 2 ♡ 7 4 ◇ Q J 6 5 ♣ K Q J

Bid 3♠, not 4♠. You have no aces or intermediates,
and weak trumps. Be content to invite game.

6. ♠ K 10 8 7 ♡ 6 4 ◇ A J 9 7 5 ♣ 6 3

Bid 4♠, not 3♠. Two nice suits and two short suits
will make this an attractive dummy in a spade contract.

No Man's Land

With a long suit, avoid ending up in 2NT.
If your hand is not strong enough for 3NT,
prefer to play a partscore in your suit.

Hands with long suits (6+ cards) are unlikely to make precisely eight tricks in notrump. If your long suit sets up, you'll probably make 3NT. If the suit does not work out, you probably will not even make 2NT.

Gambling for 3NT is one thing, but no one needs a "gambling 2NT" when a safer contract is available. Even at matchpoints, the small reward does not justify the considerable risk. With a long suit, it's easier to take nine tricks in a suit contract than eight in notrump.

West	North	East	South
—	—	—	1♣
Pass	1♥	Pass	2♣
Pass	2NT	Pass	???

♠ A 8 5   ♥ 8 3   ◇ A 7   ♣ K Q 10 7 5 3
Bid 3NT. No guarantees, but raising to game is clear-cut with this nice hand.

♠ K J 3   ♥ 5   ◇ K Q J   ♣ Q 10 9 8 6 5
Bid 3♣. You're not strong enough to raise to 3NT. With clubs as trumps, you'll have time to set up your weak, long suit.

LOOK MA, NO STOPPER

When an opponent bids a suit, you need a stopper in his suit to bid notrump. Nevertheless...

On some competitive auctions, you might have no alternative to bidding 1NT or 2NT without a stopper in the opponent's suit.

The common thread in auctions where "I was stuck bidding notrump despite no stopper" is that your RHO has just passed. If your partner has made a forcing bid, a pass by you is out of the question.

Here are a few examples. You are always South.

1.	*West*	*North*	*East*	*South*
	—	—	—	1♣
	1♡	Dbl	Pass	???

♠ A K ♡ 6 5 4 2 ◇ K 6 4 ♣ K 4 3 2

In response to partner's Negative Double, you must bid 1NT. What else can you do?

If you think that things couldn't get any worse, I'm afraid they could. If West had jumped to 2♡ and partner had doubled, you'd have to bid 2NT!

2.

	West	North	East	South
	1♣	1♠	Pass	???

♠ J ♡ A K 6 3 ◇ A 7 5 3 ♣ 6 5 4 2

Bid 1NT. Partner's overcall is not forcing, but game is still quite possible. Bidding 2◇ or 2♡ would show a longer suit, so 1NT is your best option despite not having a club stopper.

When partner may have been forced into making a notrump bid after an enemy overcall, you can't be sure if he has a stopper in that suit. You certainly don't want to end up in 3NT and watch an opponent run his suit. **Is there any way to make sure that partner has a stopper? Yes there is; the answer is a cue-bid.** This "asking for a stopper" cue-bid is sometimes referred to as a Western Cue-Bid.

3.

	West	North	East	South
	—	1◇	2♠	Dbl
	Pass	2NT	Pass	???

♠ 7 5 ♡ K 7 6 4 ◇ A J 10 4 ♣ A K J

Instead of bidding 3NT, cue-bid 3♠. Partner will bid 3NT with a stopper. If he lacks one, he'll retreat, and you will then bid 5◇.

HE SAID, SHE SAID

West	West	East	East
♠ A K Q	2♣	2◇	♠ J 4
♡ 6 4 3	2NT	3◇*	♡ Q J 10 9 5
◇ K Q J	3♡	3NT	◇ 6 5 3 2
♣ A K 9 8	Pass		♣ 5 2

*transfer to hearts

The opponents led spades. West had 5 tricks in the black suits, and developing 2 diamond tricks was easy. But when the defenders held up their heart honors, declarer was limited to 1 heart trick – down one.
As soon as the last card was played, the not-so-gentle post-mortem began. What follows might remind you of an episode from "The Odd Couple."

East: "You had three hearts! What's wrong with you? How could you not bid 4♡ over 3NT? Don't you know how to play Jacoby Transfers?"

West: "Of course I do. You gave me a choice between hearts and notrump. With three small hearts and plenty of stoppers in the other suits, I thought nine tricks would be easier than 10."

East: "No one asked you to think. When partner transfers, always play in the major with a fit."

West: "Usually I do. But with my flat hand, I thought there'd be no advantage to playing in a suit contract. If you had shown your other suit, I would have bid 4♡."

East: "If you think I should have bid 4◇ instead of 3NT, you're nuts."

Marty Sez: Clearly, the silliest comment was West's suggestion that East bid 4◇. I do think that West made some valid points, and understand her pass of 3NT. However, when partner transfers and you have three cards in his suit, almost always, "support with support."

On the other hand, whether or not you agree with West's pass of 3NT, consider the following. If West had been dealt ♡Ax or Kx, she definitely would pass 3NT. With dummy having no entries, correct defense would have limited declarer to *one* heart trick in 3NT. However, if hearts were trump, E-W are guaranteed to win *four* heart tricks. **Therefore, with his chunky 5-card suit and no outside entry, East should have insisted on playing in hearts.**

In assessing responsibility for reaching the wrong contract, I'd assign 75% to East and 25% to West.

P.S. More important than East's imperfect bidding, in my opinion, he could use a refresher course in manners.

Everyone knows: "Once you transfer, never rebid a 5-card suit." But, with a strong suit and good shape, "never say never."

Partner opens 2NT and you hold:

♠ K Q J 9 8   ♡ —   ◇ 7 6 4 3   ♣ 6 5 3 2

I hope you would agree that:

- You have no interest in 3NT.
- You have no interest in five of a minor.
- Even if partner has two small spades,
  4♠ rates to be the best contract for your side.

Therefore, transfer to 3♠, and then raise opener to 4♠. If you play Texas Transfers, jump directly to 4♡.

On the next two hands, partner has opened 1NT.

♠ 7   ♡ K J 10 9 4   ◇ 6 5   ♣ Q 9 7 5 4
If you transfer to hearts and bid clubs, you'd be forcing to game. This hand isn't worth more than an invitation. After you transfer to 2♡, raise to 3♡.

♠ A Q J 10 6   ♡ 8   ◇ J 6 5 3 2   ♣ 9 2
Transfer to spades, then bid 4♠. (If playing Texas Transfers, bid 4♡ over 1NT.) Regardless of what partner has, 4♠ should be the best contract.

Chapter 3:

Opener's Big Hands

QUIZ – AFTER OPENER'S JUMP RAISE

West	North	East	South
Pass	1◇	Pass	1♡
Pass	3♡	Pass	???

North's nonforcing jump promises four hearts and a hand worth about 17-18 points including distribution. More often than not, he'll have an unbalanced hand.

As South, reevaluate your hand and decide what to do. Neither side is vulnerable.

1. ♠ 6 3   ♡ K Q 10 9 5   ◇ 8 6   ♣ 8 7 4 2

2. ♠ Q 6   ♡ J 6 5 3   ◇ J 5 2   ♣ K J 5 3

3. ♠ K Q 10   ♡ Q 6 4 2   ◇ 8 5 3   ♣ K J 10

4. ♠ A 8 7 3   ♡ A 10 8 6 5 3   ◇ 7 5   ♣ 5

5. ♠ 8 6 4   ♡ A K J 6 5 3   ◇ Q 3   ♣ K 4

6. ♠ 9   ♡ K 9 8 6 5 4 2   ◇ K Q 10   ♣ A 2

West	North	East	South
Pass	1♦	Pass	1♡
Pass	3♡	Pass	???

1. ♠ 6 3 ♡ K Q 10 9 5 ♦ 8 6 ♣ 8 7 4 2

Bid 4♡. Your strong 5-card trump suit and two doubletons are enough to accept partner's invitation.

2. ♠ Q 6 ♡ J 6 5 3 ♦ J 5 2 ♣ K J 5 3

Pass. You have terrible trumps and no intermediates, and virtually all of your honors are as soft as butter.

3. ♠ K Q 10 ♡ Q 6 4 2 ♦ 8 5 3 ♣ K J 10

Bid 3NT. Your black-suit stoppers and flat hand suggest notrump. If partner's hand is balanced, he'll be happy to oblige. If not, you'll play in 4♡.

4. ♠ A 8 7 3 ♡ A 10 8 6 5 3 ♦ 7 5 ♣ 5

Bid 3♠. Some players see 8 HCP and bid 4♡. I see a 6-4 hand with 2 aces and a singleton, and think of slam.

5. ♠ 8 6 4 ♡ A K J 6 5 3 ♦ Q 3 ♣ K 4

Bid 4♣. Cue-bid your club control to tell partner that you're interested in slam. Bypassing 3♠ will deny a spade control. **Cue-bidding second-round controls is a must for good slam bidding.**

6. ♠ 9 ♡ K 9 8 6 5 4 2 ♦ K Q 10 ♣ A 2

Bid 4NT with this perfect Blackwood hand.

West				West	East		East
♠ A 8				2♣	2◊*		♠ 7 4 2
♡ A K Q J 9				2♡	2NT		♡ 6 4
◊ A 5 2				3NT	Pass		◊ 10 7 3
♣ A J 6							♣ K Q 9 8 2

*waiting bid

Slam was cold in clubs, hearts, or notrump. Before reading on, what do *you* think went wrong?

Here's my analysis of the auction.

2♣: Obviously correct.

2◊: Correct. Not strong enough for 3♣.

2♡: I agree. Notrump can wait.

2NT: Correct – no alternative. Bidding 3♣ would be an artificial "second negative," showing an awful hand. This convention is necessary when playing waiting bids, because a 2◊ response says nothing about responder's strength.

3NT: I agree. East did not promise very much.

Pass: Automatic.

In conclusion: No one did anything wrong. Was this an unbiddable slam? Not at all. If East had been *free* to show a good club suit, West would have insisted on slam. **What is needed is a way to do away with waiting bids and second negatives.** If you agree, please read on.

No Need to Wait

If you're not crazy about 2♦ waiting bids, here's an alternative. I think it's the best way to respond to 2♣.

When partner opens 2♣, a response of 2♦ shows at least 4 HCP and is forcing to game. With 0-3 HCP, respond 2♥.

With this approach, responder's first bid (usually 2♦) *always* conveys information, as opposed to a nebulous, "could be anything" waiting bid. Letting opener know immediately that you are not broke and are *definitely* going to game is very helpful. In addition, it eliminates awkward, artificial second negatives. "2♦ Positive" also allows players with "ants in their pants" to show values by responding 2♦, instead of rushing to bid 2NT or introducing a shaky suit because they have "points."

After partner opens 2♣ and your RHO passes:

2♦ = 4+ HCP. Game forcing. Artificial and alertable.
2♥ = Negative, 0-3 HCP. Artificial and alertable.
2♠ = A strong spade suit (5+ cards); usually 8+ HCP.
2NT = 5+ Hearts, because 2♥ is not available.
       The suit must be excellent. Usually 8+ HCP.
       Artificial and alertable.
3♣, 3♦ = A strong suit. Usually 6+ cards and 8+ HCP.

FYI: The 2♠, 3♣ and 3♦ bids are no different than standard responses.

Partner opens 2♣. What is your response?

♠ A 7 ♡ Q 5 4 ◇ A 10 8 6 5 ♣ 7 6 5
Bid 2◇. You're on your way to slam, but jumping to
3◇ would be exaggerating your modest suit.

♠ 8 6 ♡ K 7 4 2 ◇ Q 6 5 2 ♣ 6 4 3
Bid 2◇. This hand is nothing to write home about, but
it's enough to insist on game after partner opens 2♣.

♠ 8 7 5 4 ♡ 6 3 ◇ 9 7 6 5 2 ♣ J 6
Bid 2♡. Tell partner ASAP that you don't have much.

♠ A K 10 9 8 6 ♡ 7 ◇ 7 6 ♣ 9 7 6 4
Bid 2♠. Only 7 HCP? Points Schmoints! This is a suit
that you *must* talk about.

♠ 8 6 ♡ K Q J 9 7 ◇ K 10 9 6 3 ♣ 8
Bid 2NT. With two worthwhile suits, show hearts *now*
and diamonds at your next turn.

♠ 8 6 ♡ K Q 5 4 2 ◇ 9 7 6 3 ♣ K J
Bid 2◇. The heart suit is not bad, but it's not worth the
risk of getting in partner's way by bidding 2NT. **When
in doubt, allow the 2♣ opener to describe *his* hand.**

♠ 7 6 4 ♡ 8 5 3 ◇ 9 ♣ A K J 10 6 4
Bid 3♣. What could be easier?

Are there any disadvantages to playing 2◇ Positive?
Yes, it *can* lead to heart problems. Specifically:

1. A response of 2♡ (fortunately not likely):
   A. If opener has a long heart suit, he must bid
      3♡, which wastes valuable bidding space.
   B. If hearts becomes trump, the strong hand will
      be exposed in the dummy.
2. A response of 2NT:
   A. Prevents opener from bidding 2♠ or 2NT.
   B. If the partnership ends up in notrump, once
      again, the wrong hand will declare.

Therefore, only respond 2NT with a superb heart suit.
Otherwise, responder should bid 2◇ and show his
hearts later.

In Conclusion:
Am I confident that the advantages of 2◇ Positive
outweigh the disadvantages? Absolutely.

Does everyone who tries 2◇ Positive like it?
No, only about 90%.

Is this convention "for experts only?"
Absolutely not. 2◇ Positive has helped many players
bid more accurately after a 2♣ opening bid. Unless
you're already very happy with your 2♣ auctions, why
not give 2◇ Positive a chance?

West	North	East	South
Pass	1◇	Pass	1♠
Pass	3◇	Pass	???

Opener's invitational jump promises 6-7 strong diamonds and more than a minimum opening bid.

As responder, you are allowed to pass, but if you do accept partner's invitation, **any bid you make here is forcing to game.** As always, you should strive for 3NT rather than five of a minor.

As South, reevaluate your hand and decide what to do. Your side is vulnerable, the opponents are not.

1. ♠ K 7 5 4 ♡ Q 3 2 ◇ Q ♣ A 9 6 4 2

2. ♠ 9 7 6 4 3 2 ♡ K 8 6 ◇ — ♣ Q J 4 3

3. ♠ A K 10 9 3 ♡ 8 5 ◇ J 10 6 4 ♣ A 4

4. ♠ Q 7 6 5 4 2 ♡ K 5 ◇ K 4 ♣ Q J 8

5. ♠ A J 10 8 7 ♡ K Q 10 ◇ J 7 2 ♣ 6 3

6. ♠ A K Q J ♡ 8 5 4 ◇ Q 5 4 ♣ 7 5 3

West	North	East	South
Pass	1♦	Pass	1♠
Pass	3♦	Pass	???

1. ♠ K 7 5 4   ♡ Q 3 2   ♦ Q   ♣ A 9 6 4 2
Bid 3NT. You can't wait for a guaranteed heart stopper.

2. ♠ 9 7 6 4 3 2   ♡ K 8 6   ♦ —   ♣ Q J 4 3
Pass. You're not happy, so cut your losses.

3. ♠ A K 10 9 3   ♡ 8 5   ♦ J 10 6 4   ♣ A 4
Bid a forcing 4♦. You have a terrific supporting hand,
but 4NT is premature with no heart control. If partner
can cue-bid 4♡, Blackwood here we come.

4. ♠ Q 7 6 5 4 2   ♡ K 5   ♦ K 4   ♣ Q J 8
Bid 3NT. With a gorgeous ♦K and adequate stoppers,
ignore your weak spades and bid the cheapest game.

5. ♠ A J 10 8 7   ♡ K Q 10   ♦ J 7 2   ♣ 6 3
Bid 3♡. You're hoping to hear 3NT. If opener bids
3♠, you'll raise to 4♠. Otherwise, you'll play 5♦.

6. ♠ A K Q J   ♡ 8 5 4   ♦ Q 5 4   ♣ 7 5 3
Bid 3♠! Your distribution says "notrump," but you
certainly can't bid 3NT with nothing in hearts or clubs.
Instead of giving up on notrump, bid 3♠, hoping that
partner can bid 3NT. If he raises to 4♠, you'll pass
and take your chances.

Chapter 4:

We Open;
They Overcall

Dear Marty: We missed a cold game last night. My partner told me I made a big mistake when I passed her vulnerable 2♡ bid. Was she correct?

Doris - Laguna Beach, CA

North (Doris)
♠ Q 8 7
♡ J 3 2
♢ A J 9
♣ K Q 4 3

South
♠ A J 10
♡ K Q 10 8 5 4
♢ 7
♣ J 7 2

West	North	East	South
Pass	1♣	1NT	2♡
All Pass			

Dear Doris: With your minimum opening bid, I agree with your pass of 2♡. South's bid was not forcing, nor even invitational. The 2♡ bid showed a modest hand that hoped to make 8 tricks. South should have doubled 1NT for penalties. If everyone passed, she would lead the ♡K and clean up. If an opponent ran to 2♢, South could jump in hearts to force you to bid.

After partner opens and your RHO overcalls 1NT, your only strong action is a penalty double.

When your partner has shown some strength by opening the bidding, you can double a 1NT overcall for penalties with as few as 9 HCP. If you have at least 9 HCP, you know that your side has more than half the deck. If you bid rather than double, partner will know that you have less than 9 HCP. Therefore, you are welcome to bid (or even jump) with distributional hands. **Any time you have good shape, defending 1NT should not be your first choice.**

West	North	East	South
—	1◇	1NT	???

♠ J 10 9 6   ♡ Q 6 4   ◇ K 4   ♣ A 7 5 2
Double and lead the ♠J. You don't have to worry about where your tricks are coming from. The key is that E-W have no chance to take seven tricks based on partner's opening bid and your 10 HCP.

♠ 5   ♡ 7 6   ◇ 7 4 2   ♣ Q J 10 9 6 5 4
Preempt 3♣. Make them search for their major-suit fit(s) at the three level.

♠ Q 7 4 3   ♡ K 7 4 2   ◇ 4   ♣ K 7 5 2

Pass. Your side may very well have a fit, but there is no way to find out. You are not obligated to respond with 8 HCP after an opponent's overcall.

♠ Q 8 6 5 2   ♡ 4 3   ◇ J 10 3 2   ♣ A 7

Bid 2◇. Your spades are too weak to bid. What if partner has a singleton? However, he almost certainly has 4+ diamonds, so compete in your known fit.

♠ K Q 10 9 7 6   ♡ 4 3   ◇ 8 6   ♣ 8 5 3

Bid 2♠. You would be happy to play in 2♠, or push the opponents to the three level. Even if partner has only a singleton spade, your suit is strong enough to survive on its own.

♠ 5 3   ♡ J 7 5 4 2   ◇ 9   ♣ A Q 10 9 7

Bid 2♣. The clubs are excellent, but your hearts are not. Your nonforcing bid may very well end the auction, so bid your stronger suit in case partner has to pass without a fit.

By the way: We all know players who incorrectly treat responder's double as negative after a 1NT overcall. This is definitely not standard, and is alertable. I don't recommend it, because **Negative Doubles should only be played after a natural overcall in a suit.**

AFTER AN OVERCALL IN A SUIT

Here is a list of responder's options after the opponents overcall in a suit.

West	North	East	South
—	1♣	1♠	???

Pass: Often weak, but may contain a hand with length and strength in spades (trap pass) or a moderate hand with diamonds that's not strong enough to bid 2◇.

Negative Double: Shows at least four hearts and at least 6 HCP (no upper limit). The double does *not* also promise diamonds.

1NT: 7-10 HCP, with 1+ spade stopper. 1NT denies four hearts, because no Negative Double was made.

2♣: 6-10 points including distribution. At least 4-card support for clubs, usually with fewer than 4 hearts (no Negative Double).

2◇: 10+ HCP. Usually 5+ diamonds, but 4 is possible. With long diamonds, the hand could include 4 hearts.

2♡: 10+ HCP and 5+ hearts.

2♠ Cue-Bid: Shows a nice hand with good club support (preferably five cards). Some partnerships treat the cue-bid as game-forcing; others do not. This bid denies four hearts, but says nothing about spades.

2NT: This jump shows a reasonable hand with at least one spade stopper. Some partnerships treat the bid as game-forcing (13+ HCP), while most agree that it is invitational (11-12 HCP). The bid denies four hearts.

3♣: Some partnerships treat this bid as a limit raise, inviting game. Raising opener's minor would also deny four hearts (no Negative Double). Many experienced players define the jump raise in competition as a weak jump raise (WJR).

3◇, 3♡: I strongly recommend that you play weak jump-shifts (WJS) in competition. Responder shows a very weak hand with a strong 6 or 7-card suit.

3NT: Shows two spade stoppers with enough strength to insist on game. Denies four hearts.

4♡: Preemptive with an independent heart suit.

By the way #1: Nothing addressed on these two pages needs to be alerted.

By the way #2: The most important issue for every partnership is that both players are in agreement as to what each bid shows.

QUIZ — AFTER RHO OVERCALLS

On each of these hands, the auction has begun:

West	North	East	South
Pass	1♣	1♠	???

As South, evaluate your hand and decide what to do. Only your side is vulnerable.

1. ♠ 7 4 ♡ A J 7 4 ◇ Q 10 9 6 ♣ Q 8 3
2. ♠ 7 4 2 ♡ A J 7 4 3 ◇ 6 5 ♣ K 6 3
3. ♠ 6 5 ♡ A K J ◇ J 7 6 5 4 ♣ 8 7 5
4. ♠ 6 5 3 ♡ J 10 9 5 ◇ 4 ♣ A K 7 5 4
5. ♠ A Q J ♡ 7 6 4 3 ◇ Q 9 8 ♣ 8 4 2
6. ♠ 6 3 ♡ A 9 2 ◇ A Q 5 ♣ K 9 8 7 4
7. ♠ A 5 ♡ A K 7 5 ◇ 9 6 5 4 ♣ A Q 5
8. ♠ 7 ♡ A J 9 8 ◇ Q 10 9 6 4 3 ♣ 8 3
9. ♠ 7 ♡ A J 9 8 ◇ A Q 10 8 6 3 ♣ K 3
10. ♠ 7 ♡ A J 9 8 ◇ J 7 6 3 2 ♣ A K 3
11. ♠ 7 6 5 3 ♡ A K ◇ K J 7 5 ♣ 8 4 2
12. ♠ 6 ♡ K Q J 10 8 7 6 5 ◇ 4 2 ♣ 5 4
13. ♠ K Q 10 8 7 ♡ J 6 5 3 ◇ K 3 2 ♣ 3
14. ♠ 8 6 3 ♡ 9 ◇ K Q J 9 7 6 5 ♣ 8 4
15. ♠ A 7 ♡ A K Q J 3 ◇ 8 7 2 ♣ K 8 2
16. ♠ K J 7 ♡ K 9 ◇ 6 5 4 3 2 ♣ A Q 10
17. ♠ 7 5 3 ♡ A Q ◇ 8 7 6 5 ♣ J 10 8 6

1. ♠ 7 4 ♡ A J 7 4 ◇ Q 10 9 6 ♣ Q 8 3
Double. This is as perfect a Negative Double as you
are likely to pick up. Enjoy it while you can – most
hands are a lot more gray than black and white.

2. ♠ 7 4 2 ♡ A J 7 4 3 ◇ 6 5 ♣ K 6 3
Double. This is a typical *imperfect* Negative Double.
You want to show your hearts while it is easy to do so.
Of course, partner won't know about your fifth heart.
Not having diamonds is not a problem, because
Negative Doubles never guarantee the unbid minor.

3. ♠ 6 5 ♡ A K J ◇ J 7 6 5 4 ♣ 8 7 5
Double. A *very* imperfect Negative Double; however,
every other action is even less appealing. Once partner
opened, you'd like to compete. If opener bids a 4-card
heart suit, he won't hate your ♡A K J.

4. ♠ 6 5 3 ♡ J 10 9 5 ◇ 4 ♣ A K 7 5 4
Double. You expect to support partner's clubs, but
first tell him about your 4-card major. If you don't
find a heart fit, you're ready, willing, and able to
support clubs later.

5. ♠ A Q J ♡ 7 6 4 3 ◇ Q 9 8 ♣ 8 4 2
Bid 1NT. Your bid denies four hearts, but with *three*
spade stoppers and a totally flat hand, concealing *this*
major is sensible.

West	North	East	South
Pass	1♣	1♠	???

6. ♠ 6 3   ♡ A 9 2   ◇ A Q 5   ♣ K 9 8 7 4
Cue-Bid 2♠. This promises a good hand in support
of clubs.

7. ♠ A 5   ♡ A K 7 5   ◇ 9 6 5 4   ♣ A Q 5
Double. **A Negative Double does not deny a
strong hand.** You have all the time in the world.

8. ♠ 7   ♡ A J 9 8   ◇ Q 10 9 6 4 3   ♣ 8 3
Double. If North rebids 1NT, you'll correct to
diamonds. **A Negative Double followed by a
new suit shows a long suit but a weak hand.**

9. ♠ 7   ♡ A J 9 8   ◇ A Q 10 8 6 3   ♣ K 3
Bid 2◇. If you double 1♠, any subsequent diamond
bid would show a weak hand such as #8. You intend
to bid hearts at your next turn.

10. ♠ 7   ♡ A J 9 8   ◇ J 7 6 3 2   ♣ A K 3
Double. You're on your way to game, but you don't
need to show *this* diamond suit.

11. ♠ 7 6 5 3   ♡ A K   ◇ K J 7 5   ♣ 8 4 2
Bid 2◇. Responding in an unbid minor at the two level
does not promise a 5-card suit.

12. ♠ 6   ♡ K Q J 10 8 7 6 5   ◇ 4 2   ♣ 5 4
Bid 4♡ with this perfect preempt. If you were
intimidated by the vulnerability, take some vitamins.

13. ♠ K Q 10 8 7   ♡ J 6 5 3   ◇ K 3 2   ♣ 3
Pass. My RHO wants to play in spades? Sounds
good to me. Letting the opponent off the hook with
a Negative Double would be appropriate only during
"Be Generous to Opponents" Week. You hope partner
reopens with a double, and you'll be delighted to pass.

14. ♠ 8 6 3   ♡ 9   ◇ K Q J 9 7 6 5   ♣ 8 4
Bid 3◇. After RHO overcalls, your jump-shift is weak.
This bid is not alertable. Make it difficult for them to
find their heart fit.

15. ♠ A 7   ♡ A K Q J 3   ◇ 8 7 2   ♣ K 8 2
Bid 2♡. You are strong enough to jump-shift, but 3♡
would be preemptive. This hand has a big future – all
the more reason to go slowly.

16. ♠ K J 7   ♡ K 9   ◇ 6 5 4 3 2   ♣ A Q 10
Bid 3NT. These diamonds are not worth talking about.

17. ♠ 7 5 3   ♡ A Q   ◇ 8 7 6 5   ♣ J 10 8 6
Bid 2♣. **You don't need 5-card support to raise
opener's minor suit.** Throw your two cents in *now*.

THE RIGHT TIME TO BID 'EM UP

If a vulnerable opponent jumps to 4♡ or 4♠ on his own, he is eager to play in that contract. Try hard not to let him.

This is especially true when you are short in the opponent's suit.

In bridge, if it's good for them, it can't be good for you. How can you tell that your opponent is "dying" to play in four of his major? **Although he was vulnerable, he jumped to game without knowing anything about his partner's hand.** He knows that there's an excellent chance that he will get the bid, often doubled. Regardless of his bridge IQ, he would not take this risk unless he was ready, willing, and able to play there on his own. After all, he could have shown his suit at a lower level. He may not have a lot of HCP, but he will **always have a very long, strong suit** with a hand that contains a lot more winners than losers.

Obviously, it is easier to be heroic when not vulnerable. However, experience has shown that striving to disturb their desired contract is worthwhile even when you are vulnerable. If an opponent's exceptional distribution will allow him to make his vulnerable game, you'll be better off bidding even if your bid is doubled and you go down two.

Here's a hand from the 2003 Spingold Championship. The teams were comprised of recognized experts. E-W were vulnerable. At both tables, the auction began:

West	North	East	South
—	—	—	1♦
Pass	1♠	4♡	???

North
♠ J 9 7 5 4 2
♡ 3
♦ K 5
♣ 10 6 5 4

West
♠ 10
♡ 9 7 6 4 2
♦ Q 8 6 3
♣ 8 7 2

East
♠ A K Q 6
♡ A K Q J 10 5
♦ J 9
♣ 9

South
♠ 8 3
♡ 8
♦ A 10 7 4 2
♣ A K Q J 3

At one table, both South and North chose to sell out, and 4♡ made four. At the second table, South bid 5♣. He would have been down one – for a big gain. When West bid 5♡, the N-S triumph was even more delicious.

This hand is from the 1993 World Championships.
I held the North cards. Both sides were vulnerable.

West	North	East	South
—	Pass	4♡	Pass
Pass	???		

North (Marty)

Contract: 4♠
Lead: ♡J

♠ A 9 5 4
♡ 3
◇ A 10 9 6 4
♣ J 10 6

West

♠ J 10
♡ J
◇ K 8 7 3
♣ A 9 8 5 4 3

East

♠ 7 6
♡ A K Q 9 8 6 5 4
◇ 2
♣ K 2

South

♠ K Q 8 3 2
♡ 10 7 2
◇ Q J 5
♣ Q 7

Unwilling to let East have his way with us, I reopened
with a double. My partner bid 4♠, and everyone
passed. 4♠ made easily, just as 4♡ would have.

Chapter 5:

We Open;
They Double

Dear Marty: Although I bid normally, we went down 800! How could my partner bid 2♣ with only 7 HCP?

Pete - Pittsburgh, PA

	North	
Contract: 2♠Dbl	♠ 10 3	
Lead: ♠8	♡ 6 5 3 2	
	◇ 7	
	♣ A K 10 9 7 3	

West	*East*
♠ 8	♠ A Q J 9 7
♡ A Q 10 7	♡ J 8
◇ A 10 9 8 6	◇ 5 4 2
♣ Q J 5	♣ 6 4 2

South (Pete)
♠ K 6 5 4 2
♡ K 9 4
◇ K Q J 3
♣ 8

West	*North*	*East*	*South* (Pete)
—	—	—	1♠
Dbl	2♣	Pass	2◇
Pass	2♠	Dbl	All Pass

Dear Pete: North bid correctly. 2♣ was weak and nonforcing. With your minimum hand, you should have passed 2♣. For more on the subject, please read on.

After the Double, it's Weak

After partner's opening bid is doubled, your non-jump new suit at the two level promises a weak hand with a strong 6-card suit.

How weak is weak? The hand should resemble a weak two-bid. Of course, with as many as 10 HCP, you could have redoubled. Therefore, 5-9 HCP is the norm.

As always, vulnerability is relevant. However, if you have a strong suit but are vulnerable, you should not be worrying: "Suppose I make a bid, get doubled, and go down a zillion points. How embarrassing!" Instead, **always be eager to compete aggressively with a good, long suit.**

Your 2-level bid is definitely not forcing, and strongly suggests that you would like your suit to become trump. Because partner may have to pass despite hating your suit, you prefer to have enough intermediate cards to survive on your own.

On the following hands, you are South, with both sides vulnerable. Decide whether or not your long suit is worth mentioning.

West	North	East	South
Pass	1♠	Dbl	???

♠ 9 ♡ A Q J 10 9 3 ◇ 8 5 4 ♣ 8 7 3

Bid 2♡. You have a weak hand with an excellent 6-card suit. The only flaw is your singleton in partner's major. Otherwise, this is a classic hand for the bid.

♠ Q 4 ♡ 9 7 ◇ 8 4 3 ♣ K Q 8 6 5 2

Bid 2♣. You'd prefer better club intermediates, but bidding now is better than passing and guessing later on. In addition, if your LHO becomes declarer in a heart contract, you definitely want a club lead.

♠ 7 5 ♡ Q 10 4 ◇ J 8 7 5 4 3 ♣ A 4

Don't bid 2◇ with this very weak suit. Some would pass, but I'd bid an imperfect 1NT in order to compete.

♠ 6 ♡ Q 10 4 ◇ J 8 7 5 4 3 2 ♣ A 4

Bid 2◇. Your diamonds still don't sparkle, but you can't ignore *seven* of them.

♠ 7 ♡ Q J 10 9 8 7 3 ◇ 10 5 3 2 ♣ 7

Jump to 3♡. With no defense and a "solid" 7-card suit, this is a perfect weak jump-shift in competition.

NOT A LIMIT RAISE

After RHO's takeout double, a jump raise of opener's suit is NOT a limit raise. It is preemptive, and shows a very weak hand.

Question: How weak is very weak?
Answer: Roughly 3-7 points, including distribution. If a minor is opened, the maximum is slightly higher. When your side is vulnerable, be less aggressive with marginal hands.

Question: How much support does responder need?
Answer: 4 cards for majors, 5 cards for minors.

Question: Does everyone play this way?
Answer: As usual, the answer to that question is a resounding "no." However, after a takeout double, a weak jump raise (WJR) is considered "standard" for both intermediate and advanced players.

Question: Does opener need to alert this WJR?
Answer: No, it is not alertable.

Question: How do you justify jumping when so weak?
Answer: The LAW of Total Tricks (LOTT). With nine trumps, you are *always* happy to bid to the three level. Without question, a WJR is one of my favorite bids.

West	North	East	South
—	1♡	Dbl	???

Jump to 3♡ with these hands:

1. ♠ 7 3   ♡ A J 10 4   ◇ 8 5 4   ♣ 9 7 3 2
2. ♠ 8 7 6   ♡ Q 5 4 3   ◇ 9   ♣ 8 6 5 4 2

West	North	East	South
Pass	1◇	Dbl	???

Jump to 3◇ with these hands:

3. ♠ 7 6 2   ♡ 6 4   ◇ K Q 10 5 3   ♣ 7 4 3
4. ♠ 9 6 4   ♡ 7   ◇ Q J 6 5 2   ♣ Q 5 4 2

Question: If a jump raise is weak, how can responder make a limit raise?

Answer: If responder has support and points, he can redouble, then support opener's suit at his next turn. Or, for those who prefer a direct approach, an alertable jump to 2NT (Jordan) shows a limit raise or better. Also, when partner opens a major suit, advocates of Bergen Raises "ignore the double" and jump to 3 of a minor (artificial and alertable) with good support.

By the way: LOTT advocates, who love to support and preempt, also use the WJR after an enemy overcall.

On the following deal, only E-W was vulnerable. They missed a cold game. What do *you* think went wrong?

	North	
Contract: 3♠	♠ A K J 9	
Lead: ♠7	♡ A K 10	
	◇ 10 5	
	♣ J 9 7 5	

West	*East*
♠ 7	♠ 8 5 3
♡ Q 8 7 6	♡ J 5 4 3 2
◇ K 9 6 4 2	◇ A Q 7
♣ A Q 10	♣ K 4

South
♠ Q 10 6 4 2
♡ 9
◇ J 8 3
♣ 8 6 3 2

West	*North*	*East*	*South*
1◇	Dbl	Rdbl	2♠
Pass	3♠	All Pass	

3♠ was down one – declarer losing two diamonds and three club tricks. In 4♡, E-W would have lost only one spade and two hearts, and scored up their game.
My thoughts on the auction are on the following pages.

West's 1♦: I like it. A real Rule of 20 hand. This bid should have helped E-W bid their 21 HCP game.

North's Double: As obvious as could be.

East's Redouble: With 10 HCP, this was very *normal*. I'll have more to say about the redouble later on.

South's preemptive jump to 2♠: an excellent application of The LAW of Total Tricks (LOTT). North promised at least three spades for his double, so there was no risk in jumping to 2♠ with the 8-card fit. This was the key bid that caused E-W to lose their heart fit.

West's pass of 2♠: West wanted to make a takeout double, but in "Standard," all doubles by the side that redoubled are for penalties (never my preference when they have a fit). It was normal for West to pass 2♠.

North's raise to 3♠: Another good LOTT bid. South promised five spades; 5+4 = 9. With nine trumps, you are virtually always safe at the three level. If you don't make your contract, your loss will be less than if you allowed the opponents to play in their best contract.

East's pass of 3♠: Would you have been willing to ignore North's takeout double (and the vulnerability), and introduce that heart suit at the four level?

West		East	
♠ 7		♠ 8 5 3	
♡ Q 8 7 6		♡ J 5 4 3 2	
◇ K 9 6 4 2		◇ A Q 7	
♣ A Q 10		♣ K 4	

West	North	East	South
1◇	Dbl	Rdbl	2♠
Pass	3♠	All Pass	

West's pass after 3♠: I'm sure he wasn't thrilled, but what else could he do *at this level?*

Yes, either East or West *might* have found a way to overcome the spade barrage. Maybe so; but I'm sure you'll agree that once South jumped to 2♠, nothing was easy for E-W. However, it could have been!

Instead of redoubling to show his points, East should have ignored North's double and responded 1♡. West would be delighted to raise, and E-W would continue on to game.

Here is a recent discussion I had with an experienced player on this very topic.

Question: What happened to redoubling with 10+ pts?

Answer: Sometimes, yes. Always? No. If your RHO passes partner's opening bid, don't you respond in a major with 6 points (or 10 or 14, etc.) without worrying about your points? While the opponent's takeout double should change *some* of your responses, you shouldn't throw away everything you know about bidding. Searching for a fit by responding in a major suit is good bridge.

Question: If I don't redouble, won't partner think I have fewer than 10 points?

Answer: No, No, NO! Your new suit at the one level shows *at least* 6HCP; the same as if RHO had passed.

Question: With 10+ HCP, how do I decide whether to redouble or bid?

Answer: If you're interested in a suit and can show it at the one level, bid it. Here are some examples:

After an auction such as: 1♣ Dbl ???

♠ J 9 7 ♡ A K 7 ◇ K J 6 5 ♣ 8 6 4   Redouble

♠ 7 5 4 3 ♡ A K ◇ K 7 5 4 ♣ 9 6 2   Redouble

♠ K Q 9 6 ♡ 6 4 ◇ A 8 4 ♣ Q 7 4 3   Bid 1♠

AFTER RHO DOUBLES

Your response to partner's opening bid is definitely affected by RHO's takeout double.

Responder's Options after RHO Doubles:

Pass: Does not deny 6 HCP.

New suit at 1 level: 4+ cards. Forcing and unlimited.

Redouble: Neither promises nor denies support for opener's suit. Promises at least 10 HCP. However, some hands with 10+ HCP should prefer to bid.

1NT: 7-9 HCP; nonforcing (no 1NT Forcing).

A non-jump new suit at the 2 level: A strong 6-card suit and a weak hand. Resembles a weak 2-bid.

Raise to 2: Virtually the same as if RHO had passed. Note: no Inverted Minors in competition.

Jordan 2NT: Good support with a limit raise or better, whether partner opens a major or a minor.

Weak jump-shift (WJS): Weak hand – good long suit.

Weak jump raise (WJR): Weak hand – good support.

By the way: Only Jordan is alertable. Everything else is "Standard," but not everyone plays Standard.

On each of these hands, the auction has begun:

West	North	East	South
—	1♣	Dbl	???

As South, evaluate your hand and decide what you would do. Both sides are vulnerable.

1. ♠ J 7 5 4   ♡ 8 7 6 4 3   ◇ J 8 5 3   ♣ —
2. ♠ Q 8 7   ♡ Q 6 4 3   ◇ Q 5 4 2   ♣ 6 5
3. ♠ 4 3   ♡ K Q 9 8 6   ◇ 6 5   ♣ 9 7 6 3
4. ♠ 8 7   ♡ 8 5 3   ◇ K J 10 9 5 2   ♣ 7 3
5. ♠ 8   ♡ 8 5   ◇ K Q 10 9 8 5 2   ♣ 7 3 2
6. ♠ 8 4   ♡ 8 5 3   ◇ K J 8 7 5 4 3   ♣ 7
7. ♠ K Q 5   ♡ A J 3   ◇ J 6 5 4   ♣ 9 8 6
8. ♠ 7   ♡ A Q 7 6 2   ◇ K Q 3   ♣ 8 7 5 3
9. ♠ 4 3   ♡ 10 7 2   ◇ J 6 5 4   ♣ A Q 9 3
10. ♠ J 8 4   ♡ K J 2   ◇ A 7 5 4   ♣ 9 7 3
11. ♠ 9 8   ♡ A 8   ◇ 8 6 5 4   ♣ K Q J 9 3
12. ♠ A K 8   ♡ 6 5   ◇ 8 6 5 4   ♣ A 9 3 2
13. ♠ K 10 9   ♡ J 7 5 2   ◇ K J 4   ♣ J 7 3
14. ♠ 4   ♡ 10 7 2   ◇ 9 6 5 4   ♣ K Q 9 7 3
15. ♠ 9   ♡ 5   ◇ 10 9 6 5 2   ♣ K Q 9 7 6 3

West	North	East	South
—	1♣	Dbl	???

1. ♠ J 7 5 4   ♡ 8 7 6 4 3   ◇ J 8 5 3   ♣ —

Pass. **It's not up to you to rescue opener.** If West has a club stack and passes the double, North can bid a suit, or force you to bid by making an S.O.S. redouble.

2. ♠ Q 8 7   ♡ Q 6 4 3   ◇ Q 5 4 2   ♣ 6 5

Pass this ugly hand. There is nothing that you are eager to say. After your RHO takes action, don't bid just because you have 6 HCP. You don't have to strain to keep the auction open in case partner has a big hand; your RHO has already done that.

3. ♠ 4 3   ♡ K Q 9 8 6   ◇ 6 5   ♣ 9 7 6 3

Bid 1♡. Now you have a suit worth talking about. Even if your side doesn't get the contract, partner will know that you'd like a heart lead.

4. ♠ 8 7   ♡ 8 5 3   ◇ K J 10 9 5 2   ♣ 7 3

Bid 2◇. A textbook example of a WJS in competition.

5. ♠ 8   ♡ 8 5   ◇ K Q 10 9 8 5 2   ♣ 7 3 2

Bid 3◇, the same bid you should make as dealer.

6. ♠ 8 4   ♡ 8 5 3   ◇ K J 8 7 5 4 3   ♣ 7

Bid only 2◇, because of the indifferent suit.

7.   ♠ K Q 5   ♡ A J 3   ◇ J 6 5 4   ♣ 9 8 6

Redouble. You have no suit worth talking about, so you're delighted to have this convenient opportunity to show your 10+ HCP. You expect to bid notrump at your next turn.

8.   ♠ 7   ♡ A Q 7 6 2   ◇ K Q 3   ♣ 8 7 5 3

Bid 1♡, rather than redouble. You'd better show your hearts *now,* before the opponents get their spades into the picture.

9.   ♠ 4 3   ♡ 10 7 2   ◇ J 6 5 4   ♣ A Q 9 3

Bid 2♣. Let partner know about your club support and modest values. Worried about getting into trouble if partner has only three clubs? Don't. Why is that?

    A. He usually will have at least four clubs.

    B. Your raise will give partner a lot more information about your hand than 1 ◇ or pass.

    C. Your bid will definitely make life more difficult for your LHO.

    D. A 2♣ bid is your best chance to get a club lead.

10.   ♠ J 8 4   ♡ K J 2   ◇ A 7 5 4   ♣ 9 7 3

Bid 1NT. You can't wait for stoppers in all unbid suits. This describes your hand in one bid a lot better than if you bid 1 ◇ .

West	North	East	South
—	1♣	Dbl	???

11. ♠ 9 8   ♡ A 8   ◇ 8 6 5 4   ♣ K Q J 9 3

Bid 2NT if playing Jordan to show a good raise.
Otherwise, you'll have to content yourself by doing
a "two-step" – redouble and then support clubs.

12. ♠ A K 8   ♡ 6 5   ◇ 8 6 5 4   ♣ A 9 3 2

With good defense but only moderate support,
redouble whether or not you're playing Jordan 2NT.

13. ♠ K 10 9   ♡ J 7 5 2   ◇ K J 4   ♣ J 7 3

Bid a descriptive 1NT, rather than a nebulous 1♡.
With 4-3-3-3 and lousy hearts, ignore your weak suit.

14. ♠ 4   ♡ 10 7 2   ◇ 9 6 5 4   ♣ K Q 9 7 3

Bid 3♣. With your weak hand and length and strength
in opener's suit, this is a textbook example of a weak
jump raise.

15. ♠ 9   ♡ 5   ◇ 10 9 6 5 2   ♣ K Q 9 7 6 3

Bid a preemptive 4♣, and leave all future decisions to
your partner. If this bid frightens you, you're my kind
of opponent.

Chapter 6:

After They Open

Dear Marty: I made a normal 4th-best lead, but my partner hated it. A heart lead would have worked great. What would you have led?　　*Dave - Alexandria, VA*

		North
Contract: 3NT		♠ A Q J
Lead: ◇ 8		♡ 9 6
		◇ A 5
		♣ A Q J 10 7 5

West (Dave)		*East*
♠ 10 7 3		♠ 9 8 6 5
♡ Q 3 2		♡ K J 10 8 5
◇ K J 9 8 2		◇ 7 4
♣ 8 3		♣ K 2

	South	
	♠ K 4 2	
	♡ A 7 4	
	◇ Q 10 6 3	
	♣ 9 6 4	

West	North	East	South
Pass	1♣	Pass	1NT
Pass	3NT	All Pass	

Dear Dave: I have no problem with your diamond lead, but I think your partner fell asleep. Regardless of vulnerability, with that nice suit, he should have overcalled 1♡. That would have made your opening lead very easy.

Good Suits Mean a Lot

If you have a strong suit, it is okay to overcall at the one level with a weak hand.

Yes, it's nice if you have something on the side to go with your superb suit – but it is not necessary. **Always be eager to talk about good suits.**

Your RHO opens 1♣. On the following three hands, what would you do at:

A: Favorable vul. (only the opponents are vulnerable).
B: Unfavorable vul. (only your side is vulnerable).

1. ♠ 10 9 8 4　♡ 7　◇ A K J 9 8　♣ 8 6 2

A. Overcall 1◇. Your diamonds are lovely, both in terms of honor cards and intermediates. In addition, your spades are chunky, and 5-4-3-1 is an underrated distribution. If you don't overcall, you can't complain if your partner doesn't make the best opening lead.

B. Overcall 1◇. With all the pluses outlined above, don't be scared to bid just because of the vulnerability. As my wife says, "If I didn't want to show off my diamonds, I never would have allowed you to buy them for me in the first place."

2.   ♠ 7 6 4   ♡ A Q J 3 2   ◇ 8 5   ♣ 7 3 2

A. Overcall 1♡. 5-3-3-2 hands are *so* flat and boring when playing in a suit contract. However, with favorable vulnerability, you don't need much of an excuse to bid, and you certainly want a heart lead.

B. Pass. Other than the nice suit, this hand has nothing going for it. Therefore, this very weak hand doesn't justify an overcall at this vulnerability.

3.   ♠ K Q J 10 8   ♡ 5 3   ◇ 9 7 6 3   ♣ 6 3

A. With this very weak hand and virtually no defense, an overcall would be misleading. Remember that **although an overcall doesn't promise an opening bid, it doesn't deny one either.**

However, with this solid suit and the delicious "feel free to bid when it's your turn" favorable vulnerability, no way am I going to pass. Is there a happy medium? Absolutely. I would jump to 2♠! Yes, I have only a 5-card suit. On the other hand, I have a weak hand with a great suit. That's exactly what is needed for a weak jump-overcall.

B. Pass. Oh well. That's why they call it *unfavorable* vulnerability.

LOWER, LOWER

The minimum needed to make a takeout double of a 1♠ opening bid is greater than what you need to double 1♣.

When you force partner to bid by doubling 1♣, he will be able to respond in any of the three unbid suits at the *one* level. No problem. However, when you force partner to bid by doubling 1♠, his response in an unbid suit must be at the *two* level. If he has nothing, a massacre at the two level may be just around the corner.

Of course, the vulnerability is relevant. It is safe to say that **when your side is vulnerable, you must be very careful doubling 1♠ with a marginal hand**

On the next two hands, neither side is vulnerable. Your RHO opens 1♣. Would you double?

♠ A 9 7   ♡ K 7 4 2   ◇ K J 5 3   ♣ 6 2
Absolutely. No matter how bad partner's hand is, it's hard to imagine getting into trouble at the one level.

Your RHO opens 1♠. Are you willing to double?

♠ 6 2   ♡ K 7 4 2   ◇ K J 5 3   ♣ A 9 7
No thank you. Forcing partner to bid at the two level with this so-so hand would be asking for trouble.

On the next two hands, both sides are vulnerable.

Your RHO opens 1♣. Are you a doubler or a passer?

♠ K Q 2 ♡ J 6 5 4 ◇ A K 4 ♣ 7 5 3

I'm a doubler. Despite the flat, boring distribution, I would take this opportunity to show some values while I can do so at the lowest possible level.

Your RHO opens 1♠. Is this hand worth a double?

♠ 7 5 3 ♡ J 6 5 4 ◇ A K 4 ♣ K Q 2

No thanks. We are vulnerable, and I have the worst possible distribution. Should I *force* partner to show his best suit at the two level, regardless of his hand? No, for now I'll pass and await developments. If partner has a worthwhile hand and *chooses* to bid, I'll be delighted to chime in later. **In competitive auctions, be cautious with balanced hands.**

Logical follow up: The minimum needed to double 1♡ (only spades can be bid at the one level) must be greater than what is needed to double 1◇ (both majors can still be bid at the one level).

In conclusion: Even at the one level, the rank of RHO's suit is very important when deciding whether to double with a borderline hand.

NO GREAT EXPECTATIONS

When an opponent opens 1NT (15-17), your side probably has no game.

West	North	East	South
1NT	2♠	Pass	???

♠ 7 ♡ K J 6 4 ◇ A Q 7 2 ♣ K 6 5 3

Pass. Yes, you do have 13 HCP; but North may need every one of them to take eight tricks. Your singleton spade will make it difficult to set up partner's suit in a notrump contract.

♠ 8 5 3 ♡ J 7 6 3 2 ◇ Q 7 ♣ A Q 6

Pass. Most of your honors are soft, so raising to 3♠ would be inviting a game that does not rate to make.

By the way: The *only* time to consider game is when you have a major-suit fit as well as excellent distribution.

With a hand such as:

♠ 10 7 4 3 ♡ 8 5 4 ◇ 3 ♣ A K 6 4 2

I would happily raise partner's 2♠ overcall to game.

On the other hand: If your opponent opens a weak 1NT, such as 13-15, 12-14, or 10-12, your side can easily have a game.

When partner makes a takeout double and RHO passes, you have to bid, so the spotlight is on you.

On each of these hands, the auction has begun:

West	North	East	South
1♠	Dbl	Pass	???

As South, evaluate your hand and decide what to bid. Both sides are vulnerable.

1. ♠ 7 6 4   ♡ 10 8 6 5   ◇ Q 9 8 7 4   ♣ A

2. ♠ Q J 10 9   ♡ 9 6 2   ◇ 5 4 3 2   ♣ 6 3

3. ♠ Q J 7 6   ♡ K 9 6   ◇ 8 5 4 2   ♣ Q 3

4. ♠ A 6   ♡ J 5   ◇ Q J 7 6 4   ♣ K 6 4 2

5. ♠ K Q J   ♡ 8 5   ◇ K Q 7 6 4   ♣ 6 4 2

6. ♠ K 5   ♡ 8 5   ◇ A K J 7 5 4 2   ♣ 7 3

West	North	East	South
1♠	Dbl	Pass	???

1. ♠ 7 6 4 ♡ 10 8 6 5 ◇ Q 9 8 7 4 ♣ A

Bid 2♡. After partner's takeout double, showing your major is the name of the game.

2. ♠ Q J 10 9 ♡ 9 6 2 ◇ 5 4 3 2 ♣ 6 3

Bid 2◇. No one enjoys bidding a moth-eaten suit at the two level, but the minimum for 1NT on this auction is at least 5-6 HCP.

3. ♠ Q J 7 6 ♡ K 9 6 ◇ 8 5 4 2 ♣ Q 3

Bid 1NT. A typical hand for a 1NT response.

4. ♠ A 6 ♡ J 5 ◇ Q J 7 6 4 ♣ K 6 4 2

Bid 3◇, not 2NT. With only one spade stopper, a notrump bid is premature. If all partner needs from you for 3NT is a spade stopper, he can cue-bid 3♠ to ask.

5. ♠ K Q J ♡ 8 5 ◇ K Q 7 6 4 ♣ 6 4 2

Bid 2NT, not 3◇. You have two spade stoppers and a diamond suit that is likely to set up quickly.

6. ♠ K 5 ♡ 8 5 ◇ A K J 7 5 4 2 ♣ 7 3

Bid 3NT. On a spade lead, you expect to take 8 tricks on your own. Partner's double showed enough strength in hearts and clubs to furnish a ninth trick (at least).

When your RHO transfers after a 15-17 1NT opening bid, there's an excellent chance that partner will end up making the opening lead. Helping him out should become your #1 priority.

West	North	East	South
1NT	Pass	2◇*	???

*Jacoby Transfer, promising hearts

As South, evaluate your hand and decide what to do. Neither side is vulnerable.

1. ♠ 8 7 4 3 ♡ 6 5 3 ◇ K Q J 9 8 ♣ 8

2. ♠ 8 7 4 3 ♡ — ◇ A K J 10 9 5 3 ♣ 8 4

3. ♠ J 8 7 6 5 3 ♡ 8 5 ◇ A Q ♣ A K 9

4. ♠ K Q J 10 6 ♡ 8 ◇ 8 5 4 ♣ 9 8 7 4

5. ♠ 8 6 ♡ 7 ◇ A Q 10 9 5 ♣ A Q 10 9 5

6. ♠ 8 6 ♡ 7 ◇ A Q 10 9 5 ♣ 10 9 6 5 3

West	North	East	South
1NT	Pass	2♦*	???

*Jacoby Transfer, promising hearts

1. ♠ 8 7 4 3 ♡ 6 5 3 ♦ K Q J 9 8 ♣ 8

Make a lead-directing double. Tell your partner loud and clear how much you love diamonds.

2. ♠ 8 7 4 3 ♡ — ♦ A K J 10 9 5 3 ♣ 8 4

Bid 3♦. With a gorgeous long suit and a shapely hand, you're not afraid of the three level.

3. ♠ J 8 7 6 5 3 ♡ 8 5 ♦ A Q ♣ A K 9

Pass. You don't want a spade lead, so an immediate 2♠ overcall has more to lose than to gain. If the opponents stop in 2♡, you will balance with 2♠.

4. ♠ K Q J 10 6 ♡ 8 ♦ 8 5 4 ♣ 9 8 7 4

Bid 2♠. There are risks here as well, but you're dying for a spade lead, so let partner know right now.

5. ♠ 8 6 ♡ 7 ♦ A Q 10 9 5 ♣ A Q 10 9 5

Bid 2NT, the Unusual Notrump, to show both minors. You're strong enough to force partner to the three level.

6. ♠ 8 6 ♡ 7 ♦ A Q 10 9 5 ♣ 10 9 6 5 3

Double. Your diamonds sparkle, but your clubs do not. A double assures you of a diamond lead. If E-W stop in 2♡, you'll balance with 3♣ to show your other suit.

Chapter 7:

After They Preempt

Dear Marty: I just hate it when they preempt. I was too strong to overcall, so I doubled and bid my suit. Not only did I go down, but we also missed a cold 3NT. A kibitzer said I should've bid 3NT, but how could I when my diamonds were so tiny?   *Jan - Los Angeles*

West	North	East	South (Jan)
—	—	3♡	Dbl
Pass	3♠	Pass	4♣
All Pass			

North
♠ J 6 5 3
♡ 7 6
◇ J 10 8 3
♣ Q 9 5

South (Jan)
♠ A K 7
♡ A 3
◇ 7 6
♣ A K 7 6 4 2

Dear Jan: You don't need nice diamonds *in bridge.* Instead of doubling, with your heart stopper and excellent hand, you should have overcalled 3NT.

When partner responded 3♠ to your double, you had a second chance. Once again, you should have bid 3NT.

NOTHING TO LOSE SLEEP OVER

After an enemy preempt, don't worry about "sneak attacks" when bidding notrump.

Consider the following hand:

♠ 7 3   ♡ A Q 7   ◇ K J 3 2   ♣ A K 6 5

The same players who routinely open 1NT with this hand become nervous about their weak spade holding after an opponent preempts in another suit. That is very impractical with a hand that feels like a notrump hand. Life is just too short for all that worrying. If an opponent opens 2♡, overcall 2NT. If the enemy opens 3♡, overcall 3NT. Sometimes, bridge is an easy game.

After a preempt, you do need stopper(s) in the opponent's suit. However, it would be ridiculous to avoid notrump just because you don't have a stopper in an *unbid* suit. Keep in mind:

- They will usually lead the suit they bid.
- The enemy doesn't know about your weak suit.
- Your weak suit may be partner's best suit.
- K.I.S.S. (Keep it simple, silly). If a notrump overcall would describe your hand well, just bid it, and don't worry.

West	North	East	South
—	—	2♡	???

With neither side vulnerable, what would you do?

♠ A Q 7   ♡ K J 9   ◇ 7 3   ♣ K Q 6 4 3

Bid 2NT. Overcalling 3♣ because you were afraid of diamonds would be silly.

♠ 8 7   ♡ A K   ◇ A K Q J 10 3   ♣ Q J 3

Bid 3NT. Your jump promises a very good hand with hearts stopped, and will often include a long minor. Partner is welcome to bid on with a good hand.

West	North	East	South
3♠	Pass	Pass	???

♠ A 3   ♡ 7 4   ◇ A Q 10 8 2   ♣ A 9 7 5

Would you:

Pass — that's awfully conservative when you probably have the best hand at the table.

Double — encouraging partner to bid hearts?

Bid 4◇ — trying for 11 tricks in diamonds?

What would I do? None of the above! I would bid 3NT without a care in the world.

After They Open 2♦

Pass: Not necessarily a weak hand. With a nice hand that had "no good bid" you'd pass reluctantly. With diamond length and strength, you'd pass happily.

Double: Takeout. With 0-1 diamond, you can shade a double. With 2-3 diamonds, you need a good hand.

2♥ or 2♠: Shows a worthwhile hand with length in the suit bid.

2NT: A natural overcall, with a diamond stopper (or 2) and at least enough strength to open 1NT.

3♣: This overcall promises clubs, with a strong enough hand to justify being at the three level on your own.

3♦: Michaels Cue-Bid promising 5-5 in the majors. After their preempt, you need at least an opening bid.

3♥ or 3♠: Not a preempt! This *strong* jump-overcall is invitational, with a good 6-card suit and 16-19 HCP.

3NT: Shows a very strong hand with at least one diamond stopper. Not necessarily balanced distribution.

4♥ or 4♠: You can't preempt a preempt! This jump promises a strong hand with an independent suit.

By the way: None of the jumps to game are signoffs.

QUIZ – THEY OPEN 2◇

West	North	East	South
—	—	2◇	???

Both sides are vulnerable. As South, what is your call?

1. ♠ Q 6 5 3   ♡ Q J 4   ◇ A 4   ♣ K 7 4 2

2. ♠ K 10 8 6   ♡ A 9 7 5   ◇ —   ♣ K 8 6 5 3

3. ♠ 7 4   ♡ A 7 5 3   ◇ A 6 5 4   ♣ A K J

4. ♠ A   ♡ A 7 5 3   ◇ A K 6   ♣ J 5 4 3 2

5. ♠ K   ♡ A K J 10   ◇ A 7 6   ♣ J 5 4 3 2

6. ♠ A 9 8 7 4   ♡ K Q 6 4 3   ◇ K 7   ♣ 5

7. ♠ 7 5   ♡ K 6 5 3 2   ◇ 7   ♣ A K J 9 4

8. ♠ A K J 9 7 5   ♡ 6   ◇ A 7 4   ♣ K Q 9

9. ♠ A Q 8 6 4   ♡ A J   ◇ A 4   ♣ K 9 8 6

West	North	East	South
—	—	2◇	???

1. ♠ Q 6 5 3   ♡ Q J 4   ◇ A 4   ♣ K 7 4 2

Pass. With this mediocre hand, don't force your partner to bid at the two or three level.

2. ♠ K 10 8 6   ♡ A 9 7 5   ◇ —   ♣ K 8 6 5 3

Double is clearcut. Shape is everything. This hand is *so* much better than hand #1 that you should have no reservations about doubling, even if East opened 3◇.

3. ♠ 7 4   ♡ A 7 5 3   ◇ A 6 5 4   ♣ A K J

Bid 2NT, which suggests that you would have opened 1NT. Bidding 2NT on your own is hardly ideal; you'd like to have a second diamond stopper, and you have no idea where your tricks are coming from. On a *very* bad day, you'll be down four! Nevertheless, with a strong hand but only two spades, both pass and double should be dismissed.

4. ♠ A   ♡ A 7 5 3   ◇ A K 6   ♣ J 5 4 3 2

Bid 2NT. Obviously, you wouldn't have opened 1NT with this hand, but no other call tempts me even a little bit. If you're starting to feel very uncomfortable, that's exactly what your opponent was hoping for when he preempted. The moral is: whenever possible, do it to them before they can do it to you.

5. ♠ K ♡ A K J 10 ◇ A 7 6 ♣ J 5 4 3 2
Bid 2♡. Treating your 100 honors in hearts as a 5-card suit should not bother you. If you have any better ideas, I'd love to hear from you.

6. ♠ A 9 8 7 4 ♡ K Q 6 4 3 ◇ K 7 ♣ 5
Bid 3◇, a Michaels Cue-Bid, promising both majors. If partner bids 3♡ or 3♠, you should pass like a shot. **Taking a preference does not promise either length or strength.** If partner has strength, he can bid game.

7. ♠ 7 5 ♡ K 6 5 3 2 ◇ 7 ♣ A K J 9 4
Bid 2♡, despite the weak 5-card suit. There is no bid available here to show both hearts and clubs. This hand is far too promising to pass, and hearts is a far more important suit than clubs.

8. ♠ A K J 9 7 5 ♡ 6 ◇ A 7 4 ♣ K Q 9
Bid 3♠. This invitational jump promises a very nice hand, because "you can't preempt a preempt."

9. ♠ A Q 8 6 4 ♡ A J ◇ A 4 ♣ K 9 8 6
Double, intending to bid spades at your next turn. The "big double" is the only way to show a 5-card suit and a hand too strong for a simple overcall.

LOWER, LOWER – ACT 2

You can double a 3♣ preempt with a lot less than if your opponent preempted 3♠.

If you double 3♣, partner can bid 3◇, 3♡ or 3♠.
If you double 3♠, the only suits partner can bid are at the four level.

1. Your RHO opens 3♣. What would you do at:
    A. favorable vul.   B. unfavorable vul.

   ♠ A K 2   ♡ J 6 5 3   ◇ K 9 6 5 2   ♣ 3

A. Double, without a care in the world.

B. Double. *You* may not consider this action to be "carefree," but with the singleton in the opponent's suit, the 3♣ preempt is not going to keep *me* out.

2. Your RHO opens 3♠. What would you do at:
    A. favorable vul.   B. unfavorable vul.

   ♠ 3   ♡ J 6 5 3   ◇ K 9 6 5 2   ♣ A K 2

A. Pass. I am tempted, but forcing partner to take action *at this level* would be going too far.

B. Pass. At this vulnerability, discretion is the better part of valor. If partner has a worthwhile hand and doubles or bids *on his own,* I'll be happy to cooperate.

Chapter 8:

Two Chances
and
Two Squeezes

Whenever possible, look for a way to give yourself a second chance.

	North
Contract: 6♡	♠ A Q
Lead: ◇7	♡ A J 8 3
	◇ 4 3
	♣ K J 6 3 2

South
♠ 8
♡ K Q 10 7 5 4
◇ A 6 2
♣ A 7 4

You're not happy with West's diamond lead. On any other lead, you'd have time to develop dummy's 5-card club suit. Even if you lose a club trick, dummy's last two clubs would provide discards for your diamonds (unless you got a very bad split).

Decide how you would play before turning the page. The opponents never bid, so you have no clue as to where the ♠K and ♣Q are located.

If you'd like a hint: take a second look at the two lines above the cards.

Contract: 6♡
Lead: ◇7

North
♠ A Q
♡ A J 8 3
◇ 4 3
♣ K J 6 3 2

West
♠ J 9 5 4 2
♡ 6
◇ Q 10 8 7
♣ 10 8 5

East
♠ K 10 7 6 3
♡ 9 2
◇ K J 9 5
♣ Q 9

South
♠ 8
♡ K Q 10 7 5 4
◇ A 6 2
♣ A 7 4

How did you do? If you immediately finessed in either spades or clubs, your 50% chance did not materialize. Too bad; it wasn't your lucky day.

The correct line of play is to cash the top clubs. If the queen falls, all is well. If not, you can fall back on your second chance, the spade finesse. By giving yourself *two* chances, your overall chance of success increases dramatically. Although it's nice to be lucky, you'd prefer to play well.

Two for the Price of One – Act 2

	North
Contract: 3NT	♠ A 6
Lead: ♠J	♡ 7 5 4
	◇ 10 5 4 3 2
	♣ A Q 4

	South
	♠ K 5
	♡ K Q J
	◇ A 8 7 6
	♣ K 7 5 3

Setting: Rubber bridge, so forget about overtricks. Your goal is to take 9 tricks.

At first glance: You have 6 tricks off the top: 2 spades, 1 diamond, and 3 clubs. Setting up 2 heart tricks is no problem, but you need 9 tricks, not 8.

Warning: This is a difficult hand. In my experience, very few play it correctly.

The reward: I consider this to be an excellent example of a hand that requires good technique. If you play the hand perfectly, you deserve to take a bow. If you don't, you'll be delighted when you learn the solution and add it to your repertoire. Plan the play before reading on.

When you saw this page, I'll bet that your first thoughts were something like: "Marty, where are the E-W cards? After your big buildup on the previous page, how come you didn't let us see if we made the hand?"

Patience, dear readers. I'm sure you'll agree that learning to play hands correctly is more important than choosing the second-best line of play and getting lucky.

I hope that you'll soon understand why the distribution of the E-W cards does not matter!

{N-S cards repeated for convenience}

North

Contract: 3NT   ♠ A 6

Lead: ♠J   ♡ 7 5 4

♢ 10 5 4 3 2

♣ A Q 4

South

♠ K 5

♡ K Q J

♢ A 8 7 6

♣ K 7 5 3

Okay, here we go. You have six top tricks that don't need to be *developed* – three clubs, two spades and one diamond. If you get lucky and clubs split 3-3, your fourth club will bring you up to seven tricks.

If you succeed in winning four club tricks, then you need only two additional tricks to come to nine. You'll now shift your attention to hearts. Once you knock out the ♡A, you're ready to score up your game.

However, if the opponents' six clubs don't divide 3-3, you still need three additional tricks to come to nine. Obviously, you can set up only *two* tricks in hearts. But you *can* get three additional tricks in diamonds *if* the four missing diamonds happen to divide 2-2.

It doesn't matter where you win the opening spade lead. Once you do, test clubs to discover where you stand. If clubs divide 3-3, work on hearts. Otherwise, attack diamonds and pray that they split 2-2.

Unless you play clubs first, you can't possibly know which red suit to attack. The technique of testing a suit to learn more about how to proceed is an example of a "discovery play."

DO YOU BELIEVE IN MIRACLES?

If declarer runs all of his trumps, on some hands, a loser may *disappear*.

One of the most glamorous declarer techniques is the squeeze. Unfortunately, too many players believe themselves incapable of executing such an "advanced" strategy. Truth be told, it ain't necessarily so. Take a look at the following deal:

Contract: 4♠
Lead: ♡A

North
♠ Q 3 2
♡ 6 5 4 2
♢ 6 5
♣ A 10 6 4

West
♠ 7
♡ A K 10 3
♢ J 10 7 4
♣ K 9 7 5

East
♠ J 10
♡ 9 8
♢ K Q 9 8 3 2
♣ J 8 3

South
♠ A K 9 8 6 5 4
♡ Q J 7
♢ A
♣ Q 2

West	North	East	South
—	—	—	1♠
Dbl	2♠	3♢	4♠
All Pass			

The defense took the first three tricks as follows: West led the ♡A, and East signaled with the ♡9. West continued with the ♡K, and led the ♡3 for East to ruff. South needed the rest, but knew that West still had a higher heart than dummy's ♡6. A club loser seemed inevitable, but declarer didn't give up. He won East's ◇K with his ace, and drew the last two trumps. He then ran his trumps.

Here was the position before South led his last trump.

                    North
                    ♡ 6
                    ♣ A 10
West   *East*
♡ 10   ◇ Q
♣ K 9   ♣ J 8
                    South
                    ♠ 4
                    ♣ Q 2

South led the ♠4 – West was not having a good time. He hoped his partner held the ♣Q, so he correctly discarded his ♣9. When West didn't discard the ♡10, declarer discarded dummy's ♡6. East's hand was irrelevant; declarer was playing "2 against 1." At trick 12, South led the ♣2 and smiled when he saw West's king. Yes, miracles (and squeezes) *can* happen.

After getting "no cards" all day, you're thrilled to see:

♠ A K Q J 5 3   ♡ K 2   ◇ K 7 3   ♣ A J

When partner opens 1♡, you can hardly control yourself. You jump-shift to 2♠, and partner raises to 3♠. With controls in all suits, you're happy to bid 4NT. Partner obliges by showing two aces, so you continue with 5NT. You're disappointed when partner has no kings, but he must have more than the two aces for his opening bid, so you jump to 7♠. The ◇J is led, and partner tables his light opening bid.

North
♠ 10 9 8
♡ A J 9 6 5
◇ A Q 2
♣ 10 4

South (You)
♠ A K Q J 5 3
♡ K 2
◇ K 7 3
♣ A J

West	North	East	South (You)
Pass	1♡	Pass	2♠
Pass	3♠	Pass	4NT
Pass	5♡	Pass	5NT
Pass	6♣	Pass	7♠
All Pass			

7♠ is an excellent contract. You have 12 tricks off the top, and can set up hearts for your 13th. To preserve entries to dummy, you make sure to win the diamond in your hand. You draw trumps in three rounds, and cash the ♡K and lead a heart to the ace. Disaster! West shows out on the second heart. You are crushed.

Your first grand slam in weeks, and now it's down the drain. Darn it! In case East is asleep, you try the ♡9, but East sneers and covers with the ♡10. You ruff and run all your trumps. Maybe East will throw away his ♡Q, ha ha ha. Once your spades are gone, you lead the ◇3 to dummy's queen. With three cards remaining, here is the position:

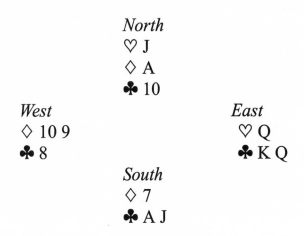

North
♡ J
◇ A
♣ 10

West
◇ 10 9
♣ 8

East
♡ Q
♣ K Q

South
◇ 7
♣ A J

You cash dummy's ◇A, and are surprised when East, who now looks like he's taken ill, discards the ♣Q. When you lead the ♣10, East plays the king. Yesssssss! You win the ♣A, and your ♣J is now good. **As long as you cash your winners and have entries to each hand, miracles can happen.**

Here is the entire deal:

North

Contract: 7♠
Lead: ◇J

♠ 10 9 8
♡ A J 9 6 5
◇ A Q 2
♣ 10 4

West

♠ 6 4 2
♡ 7
◇ J 10 9 5
♣ 8 6 5 3 2

East

♠ 7
♡ Q 10 8 4 3
◇ 8 6 4
♣ K Q 9 7

South

♠ A K Q J 5 3
♡ K 2
◇ K 7 3
♣ A J

Chapter 9:

Creating Extra Tricks

A Tip You Can Take to the Bank

When in doubt, declarer should develop his own longest side suit.

Early in my bridge career, I was fortunate enough to come across this tip in a bridge column. I can honestly say that in a lifetime of playing bridge, it is the most helpful tip on declarer play that I've ever encountered!

On the following hand, can you make eight tricks after West's annoying trump lead?

Contract: 2♦
Lead: ♦5

North
♠ J 7 6 4 3
♡ Q
♦ Q J 7
♣ J 6 5 3

South
♠ Q
♡ 10 6 5 4 3
♦ A K 10 9 2
♣ A 9

You have five trump winners and the ♣A, so you need two additional tricks. One heart ruff will be easy, but West's trump lead prevents you from ruffing two hearts.

You win the ♦J and lead the ♡Q. East wins the ♡A, and returns a trump. You win in your hand, and ruff a heart. You now cross back to your hand with the ♣A, draw the last trump, and lead a third round of hearts.

West wins, and cashes the ♣K. He leads a spade to East's ♠A, and East returns a spade. You ruff, but still have one trump remaining. You now lead the fourth round of hearts. West can win the trick, but your last two cards are a trump and the 13th heart. Making 2♦ – well done.

	North	
Contract: 2♦	♠ J 7 6 4 3	
Lead: ♦5	♡ Q	
	♦ Q J 7	
	♣ J 6 5 3	

West	*East*
♠ K 10 8 5	♠ A 9 2
♡ K J 9 2	♡ A 8 7
♦ 8 6 5	♦ 4 3
♣ K 10	♣ Q 8 7 4 2

South
♠ Q
♡ 10 6 5 4 3
♦ A K 10 9 2
♣ A 9

On some hands, remembering to develop your side suit is not enough – you must also figure out *how* to develop that suit.

Contract: 4♡
Lead: ◇J

North
♠ A 7 6 4
♡ A 4 2
◇ 8 7 5 4
♣ 5 3

South (You)
♠ K
♡ K Q J 10 9
◇ A 2
♣ A J 7 6 4

West	North	East	South
—	—	—	1♡
3♣	3♡	Pass	4♡
All Pass			

Talk about a revealing auction. You had an excellent 2-suited hand – until West showed a long, strong club suit with his weak jump-overcall. Knowing that the clubs were stacked in West's hand, you forgot about slam and settled for 4♡.

You have exactly eight tricks outside of clubs: two spades, one diamond and five hearts. In order to make the hand, you need to win two club tricks.

Because West is marked with six clubs for his WJO, East must be void. The keys to winning two club tricks are to make sure your ♣A does not get ruffed, and to trump a club in dummy without being overruffed. Obviously, you'll need to ruff with dummy's ♡A, so you must save that card. It's reasonable to cash the ♠K at trick two. Now what?

Contract: 4♡
Lead: ◊J

North
♠ A 7 6 4
♡ A 4 2
◊ 8 7 5 4
♣ 5 3

West
♠ 10 8
♡ 7 3
◊ J 10 9
♣ K Q 10 9 8 2

East
♠ Q J 9 5 3 2
♡ 8 6 5
◊ K Q 3 2
♣ —

South (You)
♠ K
♡ K Q J 10 9
◊ A 6
♣ A J 7 6 4

The correct card to lead at trick three is a small club!
West will win his ♣8. Many variations are possible at
this point, but no matter what is led, no defense can stop
you. Suppose West shifts to a trump. Win the ♡9 and
duck another club. West will win and lead a second
trump, but you're in control. Here's the position after
you win the ♡10 in your hand:

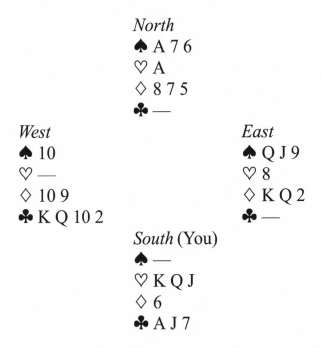

North
♠ A 7 6
♡ A
♢ 8 7 5
♣ —

West
♠ 10
♡ —
♢ 10 9
♣ K Q 10 2

East
♠ Q J 9
♡ 8
♢ K Q 2
♣ —

South (You)
♠ —
♡ K Q J
♢ 6
♣ A J 7

Ruff the ♣7 with dummy's ♡A. Cash the ♠A, and
discard one of your losers. Ruff a spade to your hand,
and draw East's remaining trump. You're finally ready
to cash the ♣A. Your last trump is your 10th trick.
Nicely done.

Although not the norm, sometimes declarer should be eager to ruff a lot in the hand that contains trump length.

Contract: 4♠
Lead: ◇J

North
♠ Q 10 6
♡ 8 7 5
◇ A 7 4 2
♣ A K 4

West
♠ 7 5 4
♡ K 9 4 3
◇ J 10 9 6
♣ J 6

East
♠ 8 3
♡ A Q 6
◇ K 8 5 3
♣ 10 9 8 3

South
♠ A K J 9 2
♡ J 10 2
◇ Q
♣ Q 7 5 2

West	North	East	South
—	—	—	1♠
Pass	2◇	Pass	2NT
Pass	4♠	All Pass	

Mission possible: Today is your lucky day. Not only do you get to see all the cards, but you also have my hint above. Can you make 4♠? Good luck.

Declarer usually does not want to shorten the "long trump" hand, because he needs to save those trumps to cope with the opponents' trumps.

Because intentionally shortening his trumps "reverses" declarer's usual strategy, this technique is referred to as a dummy reversal.

Declarer had 3 heart losers. In order to win 4 club tricks, he'd need an "against the odds" 3-3 club split. Instead, he set his sights on winning 6 trump tricks.

South won the opening lead with dummy's ◇A, and ruffed a diamond with the ♠9. Declarer crossed to dummy with the ♣A, and ruffed another diamond with the ♠J. He re-entered dummy with the ♣K, and ruffed dummy's last diamond with the ♠K.

Declarer then cashed the ♠A and led his ♠2 to dummy's ♠10. He pulled West's last trump with the ♠Q, and the ♣Q provided declarer's tenth trick.

Declarer started the hand with nine winners: 3 clubs, 1 diamond, and 5 spade tricks. Where did the extra trick come from? It's certainly not obvious.

By ruffing 3 diamonds while still drawing 3 rounds of trumps, South was able to win a *6th* trump trick.

Dummy reversals are a lot of fun. However, before considering one on "every" hand, keep in mind:

1. Make sure that dummy has enough entries.
2. Most dummy reversals require *very* strong trumps.
3. Don't get carried away with your new toy. Only a smattering of hands call for a dummy reversal.

{deal repeated for convenience}

Contract: 4♠
Lead: ◇ J

North
♠ Q 10 6
♡ 8 7 5
◇ A 7 4 2
♣ A K 4

West
♠ 7 5 4
♡ K 9 4 3
◇ J 10 9 6
♣ J 6

East
♠ 8 3
♡ A Q 6
◇ K 8 5 3
♣ 10 9 8 3

South
♠ A K J 9 2
♡ J 10 2
◇ Q
♣ Q 7 5 2

114

North
♠ A 7
♡ J 2
◇ A J 7 6 5
♣ A K 7 2

South (You)
♠ 9 6 4 3
♡ A K Q 10 4
◇ 2
♣ 8 6 5

West	North	East	South
Pass	1◇	Pass	1♡
Pass	2♣	Pass	2♡
Pass	4♡	All Pass	

After a sensible auction, you arrive in game with your chunky 7-card fit. Although 3NT would have been laydown, 4♡ is a good contract. However, West leads a trump, which means that you'll never get to ruff a spade in dummy.

You have 9 winners: 1 spade, 5 hearts, 1 diamond, and 2 clubs. If clubs split 3-3, you can set up dummy's last club for your tenth trick. However, a 3-3 split is never likely. Is there any hope if clubs don't divide evenly?

Trick 1: Win the trump lead with your ♡10.
Trick 2: Lead a diamond to dummy's ace.
Trick 3: Ruff a diamond with your ♡4.
Trick 4: Lead a club to dummy's ace.
Trick 5: Ruff a diamond with your ♡Q.
Trick 6: Lead a club to dummy's king.
Trick 7: Ruff a diamond with your ♡K.
Trick 8: Lead a spade to dummy's ace.
Trick 9: Ruff dummy's last diamond with your ♡A.

Dummy's ♡J is the 10th trick. You *must* use the ♣A K *before* the ♠A. Otherwise, West could discard his last club on the 4th diamond. He'd then ruff a club and lead a trump.

Contract: 4♡
Lead: ♡9

North
♠ A 7
♡ J 2
♢ A J 7 6 5
♣ A K 7 2

West
♠ K J 5 2
♡ 9 8 7 6
♢ 10 9 3
♣ J 3

East
♠ Q 10 8
♡ 5 3
♢ K Q 8 4
♣ Q 10 9 4

South
♠ 9 6 4 3
♡ A K Q 10 4
♢ 2
♣ 8 6 5

Chapter 10:

Little Things
Mean a Lot

LOVE YOUR INTERMEDIATES

Some players only notice honors. Better players are aware of their intermediates and make the most of them.

Contract: 4♠
Lead: ♡K

North
♠ A J 10
♡ 10 9 8 4
♢ 10 6 2
♣ J 5 2

West
♠ 8
♡ K Q J 5
♢ Q J 7 4
♣ K 9 6 4

East
♠ 7 4 2
♡ 7 6 3 2
♢ K 9 8
♣ Q 8 7

South
♠ K Q 9 6 5 3
♡ A
♢ A 5 3
♣ A 10 3

West	North	East	South
—	—	—	1♠
Dbl	2♠	Pass	4♠
All Pass			

Four losers. What else is new? Can you make West regret his obvious opening lead?

Because dummy had almost no help for declarer's minor-suit losers, the contract was in jeopardy. However, North's heart intermediates had potential. After the first trick, the defenders had only two hearts higher than dummy's ♡10 9 8.

Declarer won the heart lead with his ace, and led a spade to dummy's ♠A. South led the ♡10 from the board and discarded the ◇3. West won with the ♡Q and shifted to the ◇Q, but declarer was in control.

The remaining hearts were:

	North	
	♡ 9 8	
West		*East*
♡ J 5		♡ 7 6
	South	
	♡ —	

South won his ◇A and led a spade to dummy's jack. South persisted with hearts by leading dummy's ♡9. When East played low, South discarded his last diamond. West won his ♡J and led another diamond, but declarer ruffed.

South then led a spade to dummy's ♠10 to draw the last trump. He cashed the winning ♡8 and discarded his ♣3. He conceded a club and scored up his game.

In addition to winning the obvious six spade tricks and three outside aces, the ♡8 provided the tenth trick.

If West had shifted to clubs after winning the ♡Q, the outcome would have been no different. Declarer would play low from the board, and capture East's ♣Q with the ace. The ♣J or ♣10 would then provide the 10th trick.

{deal repeated for convenience}

North

Contract: 4♠

Lead: ♡K

♠ A J 10
♡ 10 9 8 4
♢ 10 6 2
♣ J 5 2

West

♠ 8
♡ K Q J 5
♢ Q J 7 4
♣ K 9 6 4

East

♠ 7 4 2
♡ 7 6 3 2
♢ K 9 8
♣ Q 8 7

South

♠ K Q 9 6 5 3
♡ A
♢ A 5 3
♣ A 10 3

Here's one more for the road. Can you deliver a slam?

Contract: 6NT
Lead: ♠Q

North
♠ K 5
♡ A 9 7 4 3
♢ 6 5 4
♣ 5 4 2

West   *East*

South
♠ A 6 4 2
♡ K Q
♢ A K Q J
♣ A K 3

You count your winners: 4 diamonds, 2 clubs, 2 spades and 3 heart tricks (as long as you save the ♠K as an entry to the ♡A). Your black suits are not going to yield an extra trick, so it's hearts or bust. If you're lucky enough to get a 3-3 split in hearts, you promise not to complain about anything for a month.

You carefully win the ♠A, and cash the ♡K. West follows with the ♡8 and East plays the ♡2. You lead the ♡Q and West follows with the ♡J. TIME OUT! Don't you dare play low from dummy. The sky is no longer dark and gloomy; out of nowhere a gorgeous rainbow has appeared. **You must overtake the ♡Q with dummy's ace.**

After you overtake, here are the remaining hearts.

> Dummy
> ♡ 9 7 4   East
> ♡ —   ♡ 10 6
> ♡ —

You are now on the board, and can continue hearts by leading dummy's ♡9. East can win with the ♡10, but your troubles are over. The well-preserved ♠K is still on the board, and will enable you to capture East's ♡6 with dummy's ♡7. Then, you can triumphantly win the ♡4 for your fourth heart winner, and your 12th trick.

> *North*
> ♠ K 5
> ♡ A 9 7 4 3
> ◇ 6 5 4
> ♣ 5 4 2

> *West*   *East*
> ♠ Q J 10 8 3   ♠ 9 7
> ♡ J 8   ♡ 10 6 5 2
> ◇ 10 7   ◇ 9 8 3 2
> ♣ J 9 7 6   ♣ Q 10 8

> *South*
> ♠ A 6 4 2
> ♡ K Q
> ◇ A K Q J
> ♣ A K 3

When one hand is a lot weaker than the other, declarer must be on the lookout for entries to the weak hand.

North

Contract: 3NT
Lead: ♣8

♠ Q 7 2
♡ 9 7 6 5
♢ 6
♣ K Q J 10 5

South

♠ A 10 5
♡ A K 3
♢ A K 5 3
♣ 9 8 3

West	North	East	South
			1 ♢
Pass	Pass	Pass	1 ♢
1 ♠	Dbl	Pass	2NT
Pass	3NT	All Pass	

Declarer played low from dummy at trick one, as did East. South gratefully scooped up the trick with his ♠10, and went to work on dummy's lovely club suit. Unfortunately, when East held up his ♣A until the third round and returned a spade, declarer had no way to get to dummy's clubs, and had no chance for a ninth trick.

Declarer erred at trick one when he won his ♠10. Once he did that, dummy's ♠Q was *not* going to be an entry to dummy's club winners.

From the bidding (and Rule of 11), it was clear that West held the ♠K. Therefore, South should have won the first trick with his ♠A. After that card was out of the way, it would have been easy to enter dummy with the well-placed ♠Q after knocking out the ♣A.

Contract: 3NT
Lead: ♠8

North
♠ Q 7 2
♡ 9 7 6 5
◇ 6
♣ K Q J 10 5

West
♠ K J 9 8 3
♡ Q 10 2
◇ Q 9 7 2
♣ 7

East
♠ 6 4
♡ J 8 4
◇ J 10 8 4
♣ A 6 4 2

South
♠ A 10 5
♡ A K 3
◇ A K 5 3
♣ 9 8 3

Contract: 3NT
Lead: ♡J

North
♠ K 10 6
♡ 7 5
◇ 7 2
♣ Q 10 9 6 3 2

South
♠ A Q 3
♡ A K 4 2
◇ A K 5 3
♣ J 4

West	*North*	*East*	*South*
—	—	—	2NT
Pass	3NT	All Pass	

You have 7 tricks: 3 spades, 2 hearts and 2 diamonds.
Your only hope is to set up dummy's club suit. You win
the opening lead with the ♡K. You lead the ♣J, hoping
to drive out a club honor – but both opponents play low.
You lead a second club, and East wins the ♣K.
He shifts to the ◇Q, and you win the ◇A. Once again,
you're in your hand, but you're definitely not happy.

Dummy's *one* entry is not sufficient to *both* knock out
the ♣A *and* then get back to the board and run clubs.
An entry, an entry, my kingdom for an entry.
Any suggestions?

In addition to the ♠K, the only possible entry to the board is the ♠10. Therefore, you should lead a spade and finesse the ten, and hold your breath. It wins! YES!!! It's now child's play to knock out the ♣A and claim 11 tricks.

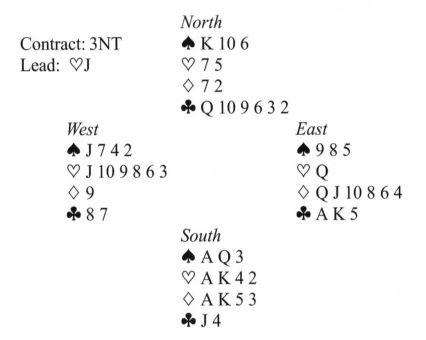

	North	
Contract: 3NT	♠ K 10 6	
Lead: ♡J	♡ 7 5	
	◇ 7 2	
	♣ Q 10 9 6 3 2	

West		East
♠ J 7 4 2		♠ 9 8 5
♡ J 10 9 8 6 3		♡ Q
◇ 9		◇ Q J 10 8 6 4
♣ 8 7		♣ A K 5

	South	
	♠ A Q 3	
	♡ A K 4 2	
	◇ A K 5 3	
	♣ J 4	

P.S. West could have defeated the contract by inserting the ♠J when you led the ♠3. That would deny you the second spade entry you needed.

P.P.S. If you *do* encounter a West who plays the ♠J, quick, check his pulse. There's an excellent chance that he's from another planet!

When declarer can guard against any division of the opponent's cards, he should do so.

This is often referred to as "a safety play."
Here's an example:

♣ A 10 8 6 (dummy)

West   *East*

♣ K Q 9 7 3 (declarer)

You have no worries unless one opponent has all four missing clubs. With your honors and intermediates, you'll be able to take five club tricks even if one opponent started with ♣ J 5 4 2 – but proceed carefully.

The key is to keep a high honor in each hand. Begin by cashing the king. If both opponents follow, they are left with only two clubs, and their jack must fall under your ace or queen.

If one player shows out on the first round, you are still okay. You know where the jack is, so you can easily finesse through that player. The 4-0 split is only a minor nuisance.

However, sometimes little things mean a lot.
Please read on.

When declarer can't guard against all bad splits, he should do what he can.

♣ A 8 6 2 (dummy)

West *East*

♣ K Q 9 7 3 (declarer)

Déja vu all over again? Not so fast. Dummy now has the ♣2 instead of the ♣10. What's the big deal, you say? Stay tuned.

Clearly, you still have no problem if the suit divides 2-2 or 3-1. But notice what happens if West has ♣J 10 5 4. Even if he shows you his hand, with his two honors *behind* your two honors, you *must* lose a trick. In that case, there is nothing you can do, so forget about it.

If East holds ♣J 10 5 4, you can deal with his two honors because they are *in front of* your two honors – but only if you keep your two honors intact. First cash the ace. If West shows out, as long as you have an additional entry to dummy, you can lead twice through East and finesse him out of both of his honors.

Suit Combinations

Knowing the best way to play a suit is essential for declarer.

The topic of suit combinations is not easy, but it is very important. Some players even find it to be fun.

Try the following: ♣ 5 4 3 2 (dummy)

♣ A J 10 8 7 (declarer)

You're in 6NT with 8 winners in the other suits, so you need to win 4 club tricks while losing only 1. You have plenty of entries, but no clues about the enemy hands.

You lead the ♣2 from the board, and RHO follows with the ♣6. Now what? There are three possible answers.

1. Don't take any finesses; just play the ace.
2. Take one finesse. If it loses, cash the ace.
3. Take two finesses. Finesse the jack now. If it loses, get back to the board and finesse the ten.

Because split honors are likely, the correct answer is to take two finesses. Your chance of winning four tricks is 76%. Taking no finesses is the worst play.

By the way: If your nine cards are divided 6-3 or 7-2, it's still correct to take two finesses.

Chapter 11:

Logical Leads
and
Sensible Signals

TOO LATE FOR ACE FROM AK

After trick one, the normal lead from a suit that includes the king and ace is the *king.*

This is recommended in both suit contracts and notrump, even for pairs who lead ace from AK on opening lead.

If you persist with leading "ace from AK" after trick one, you will frequently mislead your partner. After seeing dummy, there are a million reasons to lead an ace despite not having the king. Each time you do, unless he can see the king, partner will incorrectly place you with that card and is likely to misdefend later on. Therefore...

Leading a king after trick one is based on either:
- A suit of 3+ cards that includes the ace.
- A suit that includes the queen.
- A singleton or any doubleton except the AK.
- Occasionally, none of the above. Sometimes it's critical to let partner know you have the king.

After trick one, leading an ace denies the king.
However, with a doubleton AK in a suit contract, reverse the procedure and lead the ace first. When you then follow with the king, partner will know that you started with a doubleton and are now void in the suit.

Contract: 4♠
Lead: ♡A

North (dummy)
♠ K 10 5 3
♡ 7 6 5
♢ A Q 4
♣ K 5 4

East (You)
♠ Q J 9
♡ 8 2
♢ K 7 5 3 2
♣ Q 7 3

You are East, defending against South's 4♠ contract. Partner leads the ♡A (ace from AK), and dummy plays low. The question is: should you encourage partner to continue hearts by playing the eight, or should you discourage him by playing the two?

When this hand was played in one of my classes, East couldn't resist signaling with the ♡8. West dutifully cashed the ♡K and continued with the ♡3. East ruffed, but that was the last trick for the defense. East exited with the ♠Q, but declarer won the ace and drew trump. South then discarded North's club loser on the established ♡Q, and scored up 10 tricks.

Even if partner has the AK, don't always high-low with a doubleton in a suit contract. Encourage only if you *want* him to continue.

Contract: 4♠
Lead: ♡A

North (dummy)
♠ K 10 5 3
♡ 7 6 5
♢ A Q 4
♣ K 5 4

West
♠ 4
♡ A K 10 3
♢ J 10 9 6
♣ J 9 8 6

East (You)
♠ Q J 9
♡ 8 2
♢ K 7 5 3 2
♣ Q 7 3

South
♠ A 8 7 6 2
♡ Q J 9 4
♢ 8
♣ A 10 2

I hope you decided to play the ♡2 at trick one, because **with your spade holding, you don't need a ruff.** Once you have discouraged partner by signaling low, he will shift to the ♢J. With this defense, declarer must eventually lose a club trick, along with two hearts and your trump trick.

Dear Marty: My partner led the ♣A against 4♠. I held ♣Q6 and played the queen to start a high-low, hoping to ruff the third round. However, my Life Master partner didn't cash the king; she led a small club! Instead of going down 2, Declarer made 5! After the hand, I asked partner why she led low. She said I told her to! No, I didn't! Please help me. How can I straighten her out? *Joan S. - Troy, NY*

North

Contract: 4♠   ♠ A 9 2
Lead: ♣A   ♡ 7 6 5 3
                 ◇ A K Q
                 ♣ 10 8 2

West
♠ 7
♡ A Q 4
◇ J 8 7 2
♣ A K 9 7 4

East (Joan)
♠ 10 8
♡ J 10 9 2
◇ 10 6 5 4 3
♣ Q 6

South
♠ K Q J 6 5 4 3
♡ K 8
◇ 9
♣ J 5 3

Dear Joan: Sorry, but your partner is 100% correct. Signaling with the queen does tell partner to lead low. You should have played the ♣6. Why? Keep reading.

When partner leads a suit headed by the AK, if you play the queen, you *guarantee* the jack (or a singleton queen).

To see why this signaling method is necessary, consider the following deal. The only change from the original deal is that East has the ♣J and South the ♡2.

Contract: 4♠
Lead: ♣A

```
                    North
                    ♠ A 9 2
                    ♡ 7 6 5 3
                    ◇ A K Q
                    ♣ 10 8 2
      West                        East (Joan)
      ♠ 7                         ♠ 10 8
      ♡ A Q 4                     ♡ J 10 9
      ◇ J 8 7 2                   ◇ 10 6 5 4 3
      ♣ A K 9 7 4                 ♣ Q J 6
                    South
                    ♠ K Q J 6 5 4 3
                    ♡ K 8 2
                    ◇ 9
                    ♣ 5 3
```

The *only* way to defeat 4♠ is for West to obey your ♣Q signal and lead a *small* club at trick two. Once East obtains the lead, she can return the ♡J through South's king. That's defense with a capital "D!"

West	North	East	South
—	—	1♠	Pass
2♠	Dbl	Rdbl	3◇
4♠	5◇	Dbl	All Pass

E-W are vulnerable. As West, you hold:

♠ K Q J   ♡ J 9 7 5 4   ◇ 6   ♣ J 6 4 3   .

Partner's redouble promises a nice hand, with at least some interest in game. Because you have no idea whether your jacks are worth anything, your jump to 4♠ is optimistic. However, you love your singleton in the opponents' suit and three spade honors. When North sacrifices in 5◇, East's double ends the lively auction. Time for an opening lead. What could be easier than the top of your spade sequence? Not so fast! Think about it. Clearly, your side has the balance of power. What will declarer do for tricks? His only hopes are his trumps and short suits. So, lead a *trump*. In fact...

When the opponents sacrifice, almost always lead trump, even with a singleton.

You say that you were taught not to lead a singleton trump. That's good advice – in general. However, when the declaring side has limited strength, trump leads are the way to go.

Declarer won the trump lead in his hand and led a heart to dummy's king. East won the ♡A and led another trump. South won and led a heart to dummy's queen. He then ruffed a heart in his hand, which left him with one trump. Unfortunately (for N-S), he lacked a fast entry to dummy, to ruff dummy's last heart. When East got in, he was able to lead *another* trump.

When the smoke cleared, 5♢ doubled was down four, +800 for E-W. The ♠K lead would have allowed South to crossruff for down three, +500. E-W pairs who bid game scored +620, so the extra under-trick was crucial.

	North	
Contract: 5♢Dbl	♠ 6	
Lead: ♢6	♡ K Q 6 2	
	♢ A J 8 3 2	
	♣ K 9 8	
West		*East*
♠ K Q J		♠ A 10 8 7 3
♡ J 9 7 5 4		♡ A 8
♢ 6		♢ 7 5 4
♣ J 6 4 3		♣ A Q 10
	South	
	♠ 9 5 4 2	
	♡ 10 3	
	♢ K Q 10 9	
	♣ 7 5 2	

When your side has strength in all of the other suits, **lead trump.**

West	North	East	South
—	—	1♡	1♠
Dbl	2♠	Pass	4♠
All pass			

As West, you hold:

♠ 6 2   ♡ 5 4   ◇ Q J 10 8 5   ♣ A J 9 8

After your textbook Negative Double, your opponents arrive in game. What is your opening lead?

You're fortunate to have several attractive choices. You'd like to lead partner's major, but your diamond sequence is also tempting. Which way should you go?

Both diamonds and hearts can wait. Your side has strength in all three side suits. Therefore, if South has losers in a red suit, neither he nor dummy can have a strong suit that can be used to discard those losers.

Although you can't see the N-S cards, consider what is going on. The opponents can't have more than half the deck, so how did they justify bidding game? There can be only one answer. Great distribution.

Your mission is clear. Lead trumps early and often.

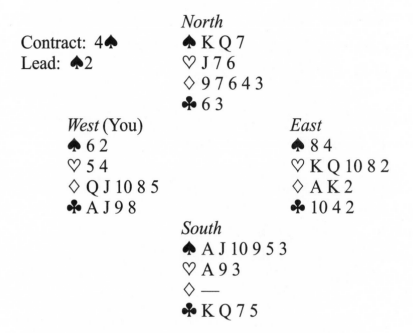

Contract: 4♠
Lead: ♠2

North
♠ K Q 7
♡ J 7 6
◇ 9 7 6 4 3
♣ 6 3

West (You)
♠ 6 2
♡ 5 4
◇ Q J 10 8 5
♣ A J 9 8

East
♠ 8 4
♡ K Q 10 8 2
◇ A K 2
♣ 10 4 2

South
♠ A J 10 9 5 3
♡ A 9 3
◇ —
♣ K Q 7 5

South will win the trump lead in dummy, and lead a club to his king. You win the ♣A, and lead a second round of trumps. Declarer's goose is now cooked. Because dummy has only one remaining trump, South can't ruff both of his club losers on the board. In addition to his two inevitable heart losers and the ♣A, he will eventually lose another club and be down one.

On any other lead, declarer would have no problems. He would win the lead in his hand, and lead the ♣K. At that point, South can't be prevented from ruffing *both* of his small clubs on the board.

If partner fails to make a lead-directing double of a Blackwood response, consider leading a different suit.

Sometimes the key clue in selecting an opening lead is appreciating that "the dog did not bark in the night."

Leading another suit may not find partner's strong suit, but at least you have a chance. Because it was easy for him to show strength by doubling the artificial response, leading the suit he failed to double gives you *no chance* to find him.

West	You	East	South
1♠	Pass	2♡	Pass
3♠	Pass	4♠	Pass
4NT	Pass	5♣	Pass
6♠	All Pass		

♠ 8 4 3   ♡ 7 5 3 2   ◇ 10 9 4   ♣ 10 9 4

Lead the ◇10 and hope for the best. If East's response to 4NT had been 5◇, and partner didn't double, you would lead the ♣10.

It goes without saying: If the opening leader has an obvious lead of his own, "never mind."

Chapter 12:

Killing Defense

Never ask your partner to do anything that you can do yourself.

		North	
Contract: 4♠		♠ K J 10 6	
Lead: ♡K		♡ 8 5	
		◇ A Q	
		♣ A K Q 10 8	

East (You)
♠ A 4 3
♡ A 9 3 2
◇ 10 9 8 3 2
♣ 7

West	*North*	*East*	*South*
—	—	Pass	Pass
Pass	1♣	Pass	1♠
Pass	4♠	All Pass	

As East, you pass throughout as N-S power into game. West leads the ♡K and North tables his very imposing dummy. Finding four tricks for the defense will not be easy. Before reading on, try to find the killing defense.

At a recent duplicate game, every South declared 4♠, and every West led the ♡K. 4♠ was defeated at only one table. Can you spot the killing defense?

The spotlight was clearly on East. He was the only one who knew about his singleton club. How could he communicate that information to his partner in time?

Some Easts discouraged hearts by signaling with the ♡2, dreaming that West would switch to clubs. Unfortunately, when West shifted, he led diamonds, and East was never able to obtain a club ruff.

The only successful East realized that there was no reason to leave partner on lead. Therefore, East took matters into his own hand. He overtook the ♡K with his ♡A, and led back the ♣7.

Declarer knew what was going on, but had nothing better to do than try to draw trumps. However, East won his ♠A and crossed to partner's ♡Q. West had no difficulty returning a club – East would have defended this way *only* if he started with a singleton club. Down one; a well-deserved top board for E-W.

Here is the entire deal:

North

Contract: 4♠ ♠ K J 10 6
Lead: ♡K   ♡ 8 5
           ◇ A Q
           ♣ A K Q 10 8

West   **East** (You)
♠ 9 2   ♠ A 4 3
♡ K Q J 7 6   ♡ A 9 3 2
◇ J 7 5   ◇ 10 9 8 3 2
♣ 6 5 3   ♣ 7

South
♠ Q 8 7 5
♡ 10 4
◇ K 6 4
♣ J 9 4 2

West	North	East	South
—	—	Pass	Pass
Pass	1♣	Pass	1♠
Pass	4♠	All Pass	

Counting to 13 may enable a defender to perform "magic."

North

Contract: 4♡
Lead: ♠A

♠ 6 2
♡ 8
◇ A Q 10 9 6 5
♣ Q J 7 5

West

♠ A 8
♡ A 5
◇ J 7 4 2
♣ K 9 8 4 2

East

♠ K Q J 9 7 3
♡ 7 2
◇ 8 3
♣ 10 6 3

South

♠ 10 5 4
♡ K Q J 10 9 6 4 3
◇ K
♣ A

West	*North*	*East*	*South*
—	—	2♠	4♡
All Pass			

On the ♠A lead, East signaled enthusiastically with the ♠9 as declarer followed with the ♠4. West then obediently led another spade. Unfortunately, the contract could no longer be defeated.

It made no difference what East led back. If he didn't lead a trump, declarer could ruff his last spade with dummy's ♡8. West could take his ace of trumps whenever he wanted it, but that's all he'd get. Even if East returned a trump, declarer could overtake his ◇K with dummy's ◇A and discard his last spade on North's ◇Q.

West had missed the boat! He should have counted spades. West had 2 spades, as did dummy. East needed 6 for his weak 2-bid, which brought the total to 10. Therefore, South must have started the hand with three spades.

Accordingly, West should have cashed his ♡A at trick two to remove dummy's ♡8. Once dummy was out of trumps, it would have been easy for the defense to take *two* additional spade tricks.

With best defense, *poor* declarer would lose the first four tricks and be down before he knew what hit him.

Contract: 3NT
Lead: ♣3

North
♠ A 6 5 4 2
♡ J 10
◇ A J 7 5
♣ 9 8

West (You)
♠ K 10 7 3
♡ A K
◇ 8 3
♣ J 7 5 3 2

West	North	East	South
—	—	—	1♡
Pass	1♠	Pass	2◇
Pass	3◇	Pass	3NT
All Pass			

You lead the ♣3 against 3NT. East tops dummy's ♣8 with the ten, and declarer wins the ace. He leads the ♡2, and you win the ♡K. Dummy's ♡10 and partner's ♡3 complete the trick. Once again, it's your lead.

You were not deceived by declarer's play of the ♣A. East can't have the ♣K or ♣Q; if he did, he would have played it at the first trick. Continuing clubs is futile; South will set up his hearts *long before* your clubs are good. What now? Count carefully. You know a lot about declarer's distribution.

Did you figure out that South *cannot* have more than one spade? He promised 5 hearts and 4 diamonds, and you know that he started with the ♣A K Q. If he has a singleton spade, it could be any card. If you're on your toes, it doesn't matter. Just in case his singleton is the queen, lead the ♠K!

When your ♠K drops declarer's ♠Q, the defense is in control. Declarer will probably hold up dummy's ♠A until the third round, but you're looking good with the ♡A and a spade winner. Nice counting, nice defense!

	North	
Contract: 3NT	♠ A 6 5 4 2	
Lead: ♣3	♡ J 10	
	◇ A J 7 5	
	♣ 9 8	

West (You)		*East*
♠ K 10 7 3		♠ J 9 8
♡ A K		♡ 6 5 4 3
◇ 8 3		◇ Q 10 4
♣ J 7 5 3 2		♣ 10 6 4

	South	
	♠ Q	
	♡ Q 9 8 7 2	
	◇ K 9 6 2	
	♣ A K Q	

When you have important information that partner can't possibly know about, tell him loud and clear.

Contract: 3NT
Lead: ♡2

North (dummy)
♠ Q 10 9 7
♡ J 10 9
◇ K Q 5 4
♣ A J

East (You)
♠ A K J
♡ A 6 3
◇ 10 3 2
♣ 7 6 4 2

West	North	East	South
—	—	—	1◇
Pass	1♠	Pass	1NT
Pass	3NT	All Pass	

You win partner's heart lead with your ace, and are happy to return his suit. However, first things first.

If you can persuade partner to lead a spade, you have three guaranteed tricks in that suit. However, there's no way partner will know that you're dying for a spade lead unless you "hit him over the head."

At trick two, cash the ♠K, making it clear that you love spades. *Now*, return the ♡6. West will win his king and lose no time in returning your spade lead. Once again, down they go. Here is the entire deal:

North (dummy)
♠ Q 10 9 7
♡ J 10 9
◇ K Q 5 4
♣ A J

West
♠ 8 5 3 2
♡ K 5 4 2
◇ 8
♣ 10 8 5 3

East (You)
♠ A K J
♡ A 6 3
◇ 10 3 2
♣ 7 6 4 2

South
♠ 6 4
♡ Q 8 7
◇ A J 9 7 6
♣ K Q 9

Sometimes, with a little bit of effort, you can figure out a lot about the missing cards.

North (dummy)
♠ 10 6 3

West (you)   *East* (partner)
♠ Q 5 4 2   ♠ 8

South (declarer)
♠ K

Regardless of whether the contract is notrump or a suit, as West, you lead the ♠2. Forget about the other suits, just concentrate on spades. The ♠3 is played from dummy, East plays the ♠8 and South wins the ♠K. Are you ready to place the missing spades?

Who has the ♠9?	East;	South would have won the ♠9 if he had it.
Who has the ♠J?	East;	Same reason as above.
Who has the ♠7?	South;	East would have played it (cheaper of equals).
Who has the ♠A?	South;	East would have played it.

So, East started with the ♠ J 9 8, and South started with the ♠ A K 7. See, a little effort goes a long way.

List of
Tip Highlights

Chapter 1 - A Whole New World

Page #

13. Rebidding a 5-card suit should be avoided when partner might have to pass with a singleton or void.

13. A 1NT response to 1♣ guarantees a balanced hand.

14. With a terrible 4-card major, 4-3-3-3 distribution, and a modest hand, responder should bypass the maj or and respond 1NT.

16. Light 1NT overcalls when non-vulnerable allow you to take action with some otherwise unbiddable hands. When your side is not vulnerable, I suggest defining a 1NT overcall as 14-17 HCP.

18. 5-3-3-2 hands are not worth much if your 5-card suit is trump. Having no long *or* short outside suits is a liability in a suit contract.

19. 5-3-3-2 is an okay distribution for notrump, or when another suit is trump.

Chapter 2 - We Bid Notrump

Chapter 3 - Opener's Big Hands

Page #

34. Cue-bidding second-round controls is a must for good slam bidding.

35. On 2♣ auctions, what is needed is a way to do away with waiting bids and second negatives.

36. I think the best way to respond to 2♣ is: a response of 2♢ shows at least 4 HCP and is forcing to game. With 0-3 HCP, respond 2♡.

37. Responder should usually allow opener to describe *his* hand first.

39. After opener jumps in his own suit, any bid by responder is forcing to game.

Chapter 4 - We Open; They Overcall

Chapter 5 - We Open; They Double

Chapter 6 - After They Open

Chapter 7 - After They Preempt

Chapter 8 - Two Chances and Two Squeezes

Chapter 9 - Creating Extra Tricks

Chapter 10 - Little Things Mean a Lot

Page #

119. Some players only notice honors. Better players are aware of their intermediates and make the most of them.

124. When one hand is a lot weaker than the other, declarer must be on the lookout for entries to the weak hand.

128. When declarer can guard against any division of the opponent's cards, he should do so.

129. When declarer can't guard against all bad splits, he should do what he can.

130. Knowing the best way to play a suit is essential for declarer.

Chapter 11 - Logical Leads and Sensible Signals

133. After trick 1, the normal lead from a suit that includes the king and ace is the *king*.

135. Even if partner has the AK, don't always hi-lo with a doubleton in a suit contract. Only encourage to tell him to continue.

137. When partner leads a suit headed by the AK, if you play the queen, you *guarantee* the jack (or a singleton queen).

138. When the opponents sacrifice, almost always lead trump, even with a singleton.

140. When your side has strength in all of the other suits – lead trump.

142. If partner fails to make a lead-directing double of a Blackwood response, consider leading a different suit.

Chapter 12 - Killing Defense

Glossary

GLOSSARY

1NT Response to Major — Refers to the standard treatment (6-10 HCP) as well as 1NT Forcing.

2/1 Auctions — References in this book apply to both the traditional 10+ HCP as well as the two-over-one game-forcing style.

2♣ Opening — A strong, artificial, and forcing bid used with powerhouse hands when playing weak two-bids. Opener either has a long suit or a balanced hand too strong to open 2NT.

4-3-3-3 — This distribution, where the 4-card suit is not specified.

5-5 — At least five cards in each of two suits.

Alertable — In duplicate bridge, some artificial calls made by a player must be "alerted" by his partner to inform the opponents that the action was not natural.

Artificial Bid — A bid that does not promise the suit that was named.

Balanced Distribution — A hand with no singleton or void, and at most one doubleton. Balanced patterns are: 4-4-3-2, 4-3-3-3 and 5-3-3-2.

Balancing Seat — A player is said to be in the balancing seat when his pass would end the auction. One should often try to reopen rather than allow the opponents to play in a low-level contract.

Bid — 1♣ through 7NT. Does not include pass, double, or redouble.

"The Board" — Refers to dummy.

Call — Any bid, pass, double, or redouble.

Cold — Slang for a contract that is sure to make.

Control (noun) — A holding that prevents the opponents from winning the first two tricks in a suit.

Count, as in "18 count" — 18 HCP.

Cue-Bid — An artificial, forcing bid in the opponent's suit. Also, a bid of a new suit after the trump suit has been established (as a slam try).

Dbl — Double.

Distribution — The number of cards in each suit.

Distribution Points — The total of a player's HCP and his "short-suit" points after a fit is found.

Draw(ing) Trumps — Leading trumps, to remove as many as possible from the opponents' hands.

Duck — To play a small card, surrendering a trick you might have won.

Entry — A holding that provides access to a hand. Efficient use of entries is crucial for both sides.

Favorable Vulnerability — You are not vulnerable, the opponents are.

Fit — A term referring to the partnership's combined assets with respect to a suit, usually trump.

HCP — High-card points.

Intermediates — Middle cards such as the 10, 9, 8.

Inverted Minors — A convention where responder's raise to two is strong (ususally 10+ HCP) and forcing, but a jump to three is weak.

Jacoby Transfer — Used in response to notrump opening bids, or a natural notrump overcall. A diamond response promises heart length, while a heart bid shows at least five spades. Opener must bid the suit responder has "shown."

Jordan 2NT — After RHO doubles partner's opening bid, responder's artificial jump to 2NT shows good trump support and 10+ points including distribution.

Law of Total Tricks ("The LAW") — You are always safe bidding to the level equal to your side's number of trumps. It is extremely helpful when judging whether or not to bid on in competitive auctions. It is based on the concept that "Trump Length is Everything."

LHO — Left-hand opponent.

Limit Raise — Responder's invitational raise from one to three of a suit, promising 10-12 distribution points and good trump support.

Michaels Cue-Bid — An overcall in the opponent's suit that shows at least five cards in each of two suits. The emphasis is on the unbid major(s).

Natural Bid — A bid which promises the suit named, as opposed to an "artificial bid."

New Minor Forcing — After opener's rebid of 1NT or 2NT, responder's bid in an unbid minor asks opener about his major-suit length. Responder usually has a 5-card major with at least game-invitational values.

Open — Make the first bid.

Preempt — A jump bid based on a long suit and a weak hand. The preemptor hopes to deprive the opponents of bidding space and make it more difficult for them to reach their best contract.

Quick Trick — A high-card holding that will usually result in a trick (also known as defensive tricks).

AK = 2   AQ = 1½   A = 1   KQ = 1   Kx = ½

Reverse — Opener's rebid at the two level in a suit that is higher-ranking than his first bid. It shows at least 17 points and promises five or six cards in his first suit. This topic causes more anxiety than any other.

RHO — Right-hand opponent.

The Rule of 20 — Used to evaluate whether or not to open borderline hands in first and second seat. Add the length of your two longest suits to your HCP. With 20 or more, open the bidding in a suit at the one level.

Shape — See "Distribution."

Side Suit(s) — Any suit other than trumps.

Signoff — A bid intended to end the auction. Sometimes referred to as a *drop-dead bid*.

Soft Cards — The queen and/or jack.

Source of Tricks — A suit which is expected to produce several extra tricks.

SOS Redouble — A redouble for rescue, as opposed to showing strength. Forces partner to retreat to an alternate contract when the partnership is in trouble.

Splinter Bid — A convention featuring a jump into a short suit (void or singleton), promising good support for partner and values for game or slam.

Stopper — A card or combination of cards that prevents the opponents from running a suit in a notrump contract.

Texas Transfers — After partner's notrump opening bid, responder can jump to the four level to transfer. 4♦ promises hearts, and 4♡ shows spades.

Trap Pass — A pass of the opponent's bid with a promising hand that includes length and strength in the opponent's suit. Used when you hope to collect a sizeable penalty by defeating the enemy contract.

Unfavorable Vulnerability — You are vulnerable, the opponents are not.

Unusual Notrump Overcall — A method of showing length in the two lower unbid suits after an opponent opens the bidding.

YBTJ — You Be The Judge.

Western Cue-Bid — A bid in the opponent's suit, hoping that partner has a stopper in that suit and can bid 3NT.

xx — Small cards; in this case, exactly two.

Appendix

WHAT WOULD YOU LIKE TO READ?

The idea for the *Marty Sez* series originated from students and readers who requested bridge tips which were easy to understand. Many of these tips were taken from material I have used in my teaching over the past 25 years.

Because there are so many more where these came from, I intend to continue writing a new Marty Sez book every year. The tips will not be repeated, and I will continue to introduce variations on the format, such as YBTJ and Dear Marty; but the practical and entertaining theme will always be present. If you have ideas for future tips, I welcome your participation. Feel free to:

E-mail your suggestion(s) to me at:
mbergen@mindspring.com
or
Mail your ideas to:
Marty Bergen
9 River Chase Terrace
Palm Beach Gardens, Florida 33418

If I do use your idea, I'll be sure to thank you with an acknowledgment and a free copy of the book.

How many times have you had the perfect hand for a convention, but couldn't make the bid because you were not playing it? Or, you were too strong or too weak to bid what you wanted to. Or, you wanted to double or cue-bid or jump, but were afraid that partner wouldn't understand you. How frustrating! The following is *not* a serious bridge tip, but with the right people and atmosphere, it's a fun way to have things *your way*.

I call it "Name Your Convention," or "Anything Goes." It's a perfect change of pace for playing bridge in a private, less-than-serious setting, but only with the mutual consent of all four players. **It is definitely not kosher when playing duplicate bridge.**

At your turn, you're welcome to make *any bid* that fits your hand. It doesn't matter if your partner has the slightest clue about what your bid means, because **you get to identify your bid out loud and, if necessary, describe it as well!**

Of course, in real life, this is too good to be true. All the more reason to have a good time while you can.

Frequently asked questions: Can you invent your own conventions? How many adjectives are allowed? Relax and enjoy - it's all up to the four of you.

Here are some examples of this tongue-in-cheek, but fun version of bridge. Neither side is vulnerable.

Auction #1. You are the dealer.

♠ A Q   ♡ J 9 3   ♢ K Q 7 5   ♣ J 10 5 2
Open 1NT, and say, **"12-14 HCP."**

♠ A Q   ♡ K J 3   ♢ K Q 7 5   ♣ J 10 5 2
Open 1NT, and say, **"15-17 HCP."**

♠ A 4   ♡ 6   ♢ A K Q 9 8 6 5   ♣ A K 5
Open 2♢, and say, **"a strong 2-bid."**

♠ 7 4   ♡ Q 2   ♢ A K J 9 5 3   ♣ 7 6 5
Open 2♢, and say, **"a healthy weak 2-bid."**

♠ 7 4   ♡ 6 2   ♢ K J 9 8 6 4   ♣ J 7 5
Open 2♢, and say **"an anemic weak 2-bid."**

♠ A K J 4   ♡ A 9 7 6 5   ♢ 3   ♣ 9 6 4
Open 2♢, and say, **"Flannery: 5 hearts, 4 spades, and 11-15 HCP."**

♠ A 8 7 4   ♡ K J 9 2   ♢ 7   ♣ K Q 7 4
Open 2♢, and say, **"Precision: a 3-suited hand with 0-1 diamond and 11-15 HCP."**

Auction # 2. Your RHO opens 4♡.

♠ K Q 8 6 ♡ — ◇ K 9 7 5 ♣ K Q 7 6 5
Double, and say, **"takeout."**

♠ A ♡ K J 9 2 ◇ A 8 4 ♣ 8 7 6 3 2
Double, and say, **"penalty."**

♠ A 7 5 ♡ 9 8 2 ◇ A Q 6 4 ♣ A K J
Double, and say, **"cards."**

Auction #3:	*West*	*North*	*East*	*South*
	Pass	1NT	Pass	???

♠ 7 6 2 ♡ K J 7 6 5 ◇ 8 6 5 4 ♣ 6
Bid 2◇, and say, **"Jacoby Transfer."**

♠ 7 6 2 ♡ 7 6 5 ◇ Q 7 6 5 4 2 ♣ 6
Bid 2◇, and say, **"natural signoff!"**

♠ A 7 6 ♡ K J 6 5 ◇ 6 ♣ A K 9 6 5
Bid 2◇, and say, **"Game-Forcing Stayman."**

♠ K Q 7 6 5 ♡ K Q 8 4 2 ◇ 6 ♣ 6 4
Bid 3♠, and say, **"5-5 in the majors, game forcing."**

♠ 9 ♡ A 9 7 6 ◇ K 8 6 5 ♣ K J 7 2
Bid 3♠, and say, **"Splinter Bid, 0-1 spades."**

CROSS-REFERENCING BERGEN BOOKS

In the last few years, many readers have asked me where they could find information about specific topics in my books. In my younger days, I was pretty good at remembering which book had which topic, and on which page. These days, I find myself forgetting, and having to waste time searching.

One day, I decided enough was enough. I made a list of some important topics, and went through all my books jotting down page numbers.

On the next five pages, you will find some of these lists. I didn't want to overdo it, so I tried to avoid listings where the topic was mentioned only briefly.

These cross-reference lists have been very useful to me. I hope that they will also be helpful to you.

Marty Bergen

SLAM BIDDING IN BERGEN BOOKS

2♣ Auctions in Bergen Books

Defense

Opening Leads

DECLARER PLAY IN BERGEN BOOKS

"We Found a Fit" in Bergen Books

Highly
Recommended

RECOMMENDED READING

Hardcover Books by Marty Bergen

MARTY SEZ	$17.95
MARTY SEZ – VOLUME 2	$17.95
MARTY SEZ – VOLUME 3	$17.95
POINTS SCHMOINTS!	$19.95
More POINTS SCHMOINTS!	$19.95
Schlemiel...Schlimazel? Mensch (not a bridge book)	$14.95

•• UNPRECEDENTED OFFER ••

For each one of Marty's hardcover books that you purchase,
mention this book and receive a **free** copy of
any one of his six most recent softcover books.
Personalized autographs available upon request.

Special Discount!

365 Bridge Hands with Expert Analysis
~~$13.95~~ only $5

Bridge Cruises with Marty Bergen

For more information, call 1-800-367-9980

Recommended Reading

Softcover Books by Marty Bergen

Buy 2, get 1 (equal or lesser price) for half price

To Open or Not to Open: *Featuring the Rule of 20*	$6.95
Better Rebidding with Bergen	$7.95
Understanding 1NT Forcing	$5.95
Hand Evaluation: Points, Schmoints!	$7.95
Introduction to Negative Doubles	$6.95
Negative Doubles	$9.95
Better Bidding With Bergen 1 – *Uncontested Auctions*	$11.95
Better Bidding With Bergen 2 – *Competitive Bidding*	$11.95
Marty's Reference book on Conventions	~~$9.95~~ $7.00

Books by Eddie Kantar

A Treasury of Bridge Bidding Tips	$11.95
Take Your Tricks (Declarer Play)	$12.95
Defensive Tips for Bad Card Holders	$12.95

NOW AVAILABLE

CDs by Larry Cohen

Play Bridge With Larry Cohen
An exciting opportunity to play question-and-answer with a 17-time national champion. "One of the best products to come along in years. Easy-to-use. Suitable for every player who wishes to improve his scores."

Day 1	~~$29.95~~	$26
Day 2	~~$29.95~~	$26
Day 3	~~$29.95~~	$26

Books by Larry Cohen

To Bid or Not to Bid - The Law of Total Tricks $12.95

Following the Law - The Total Tricks Sequel $12.95

CDs by Kit Woolsey

Cavendish 2000:		
Day 1	~~$29.95~~	$26
Days 2-3	~~$29.95~~	$26

Software by Fred Gitelman

Bridge Master 2000 ~~$59.95~~ $48
"Best software ever created for improving your declarer play."

· · **FREE SHIPPING ON ALL SOFTWARE** · ·
(in the U.S.)

ONE-ON-ONE WITH MARTY

Why not improve your bridge with an experienced, knowledgeable teacher? Enjoy a private bridge lesson with Marty Bergen. You choose the format and topics, including Q&A, conventions, bidding, and cardplay.

Marty is available for lessons via phone and e-mail. Beginners, intermediates, and advanced players will all benefit from his clear and helpful teaching style.

For further information, please call the number below, or e-mail Marty at: mbergen@mindspring.com

ORDERING INFORMATION

To place your order, call Marty toll-free at
1-800-386-7432
all major credit cards are welcome

Or send a check or money order (U.S. currency), to:

Marty Bergen
9 River Chase Terrace
Palm Beach Gardens, FL 33418-6817

Please include $3 postage and handling for each order.

Postage is FREE (in U.S.) if your order includes any CD or copy of Marty's hardcover books.